Our Journey
WITH God

Jan,

   May the Lord bless you
and keep you as you walk
with Him.

    Embrace the journey!

Joe

Our Journey WITH God

Insights for Navigating a
Willing, Intimate, Trusting and Humble Life

JOE KILLIAN

XULON PRESS

Xulon Press
2301 Lucien Way #415
Maitland, FL 32751
407.339.4217
www.xulonpress.com

Printed in the United States of America.

ISBN-13: 978-1-5456-6751-4

DEDICATION

For Maria, my loving wife
who accompanied me through more than
five years of writing this book. You are the world's
most patient editor, and I want everyone to know
just how much of your love is in each and every
word of this book.

Where I have been and where I am going, was and
is immeasurably better because I am blessed
beyond words to be on this journey with you.
(I hope I got the punctuation and tense right in this
because it's too late for you to correct it now!)

Words can't express how grateful I am for all your
love and support.
I love you!

TABLE OF CONTENTS

ACKNOWLEDGEMENTS

First and foremost, I have to acknowledge Joey, Sarah and Joshua, our amazing children. The stories in this book about each of you only begin to touch the love, joy and pride you've brought to our lives. I need you to know that my love for you is in each and every story—especially the ones about your "misbehaviors."

To Mom and Dad, you've shown me how to persevere on the journey no matter how challenging it has been. I love you!

To my siblings, Laurie, Jeffrey and PJ, who had to endure an overbearing, know-it-all, bossy big brother. Thank you for loving me despite how mean I was to you when we were young. I love you all!

Holli Luther, your steadfast faith in God has modeled for me what a journey with him is supposed to be. Your enthusiasm for this book has continually inspired me. Thank you for your loving acceptance and encouragement.

Caryn Dahm, the only thing more joyful than your beautiful illustrations is your spirit in Christ.

To my editorial team of friends: Jan Krouskop, I can always count on you to challenge and encourage me on my journey. Your comments in the later stages of editing did both. I am blessed to call you my friend. Dr. Paul Niemiec, you occupy a unique place in my story and I will be forever grateful for your wisdom and encouragement throughout the years. Don Ross, the first time I saw your edits I thought you had totally rewritten the book.

Once we worked through your suggestions I realized how much better the book became because of your thoughtful words. Lisa Barton, you were the perfect proofreader, because cleaning up my writing was a Herculean task. You did it while teaching me more about grammar and punctuation than I learned in high school—especially the use of the em dash.

Mike Aquilina, the time you took out of your busy schedule to spend with me during a particularly challenging time in my writing encouraged me more than you'll know.

I save my final thank you for God, who was, is and always will be my inspiration. I hope you are pleased with this book.

ENDORSEMENTS

This book has the power to transform lives. It's perfect for individual, group, or even whole-parish study. Highly recommended.

Mike Aquilina
Author and EWTN Host

Our ability to love, wrote Dr. Conrad Baars, "is freed when we experience ourselves as good, worthwhile, and lovable." In his book, *Our Journey WITH God*, Joe Killian helps us to do just that by inviting us to see our lives in the context of a journey, one in which we are not alone. Through personal anecdotes and wisdom garnered through living a life of prayer, Joe helps us to identify ourselves not as the falls we have experienced in life, but as beloved children of God, capable of being loved and therefore of loving. I have been blessed by reading *Our Journey WITH God*, and I know the same will be true for all others who read it as well.

Fr. Joe Freedy
Diocese of Pittsburgh, PA

Killian is a masterful storyteller who leads us through a journey to discover our own story, which starts with God, who wants to have a relationship with us, guide us and help us to discover our identity and purpose in life. If you have ever questioned your purpose—you need to read this book!

Mimika Garesché
Founder of ON FIRE Missionary Discipleship Collaborative

St. Peter tells us to "Always have your answer ready for those who ask the reason for your hope." (1 Peter 3:15) If we are going to be ambassadors for Christ we need to be able to tell our stories, our own personal stories of journeying with God in a way that weaves together with the great narrative of Salvation History. In *Our Journey WITH God*, Joe Killian has provided a wonderful and inspiring tool to help us find our place in this great story and to tell the story of our own journey.

Fr. James Mallon
Author of *Divine Renovation*
Episcopal Vicar for Parish Renewal and Leadership Support
Archdiocese of Halifax-Yarmouth, Nova Scotia, Canada

Our Journey WITH God is a thoughtful, prayerful, and delightful book. Joe Killian has written a deeply spiritual and a deeply human guide to living a spiritual life rooted both in Scripture and daily experience. *Our Journey WITH God* is personal, too. Joe's stories from his own life and the "Capture Your Moment" pauses invite reflection and action in the here and now of your own journey. When you read *Our Journey WITH God*, open your mind and heart to the Holy Spirit and be filled with hope and joy and gratitude. I was.

Dr. Paul Niemiec, LPC
Catholic Charities of the Diocese of Greensburg, PA

Joe Killian has discovered a treasure and is leaving a popcorn trail for you! Through interwoven stories of faith and family, this book is like receiving a cold drink during the difficult moments of a race. It places our story within the context of God's story, with each page illustrating the book we all must write to better accompany others on their own journey with God.

Gary W. Roney
Director, Youth and Young Adult Engagement
Diocese of Pittsburgh, PA

Since the beginning of time, the idea of journey has been a significant one for people of faith. If you are looking to deepen your faith journey, Joe Killian is a trusted guide. Through personal story, Scriptural truth, and challenging questions, this book provides the needed fuel to ensure that your journey with God is a rich, fulfilling, and life changing one.

Terry Timm
Pastor, Christ Community Church
Author, *A Movable Feast: Worship for the Other Six Days*

PREFACE

There are a lot of ways to experience a journey:

> The excitement of a new path,
> The routine of our daily commute,
> The trip down memory lane,
> The long-awaited family vacation,
> The intense traffic jam,
> The meandering stroll,
> The guided tour.

Our journey with God is no different.

Every journey has its share of starts and stops, ups and downs, twists and turns and even some detours along the way. At the same time, the journeys we take and how we experience them are as numerous as there are people. The purpose of this book is to encourage a look at our lives in the context of a journey. We are all on our own unique paths, and there are many questions to be answered along the way.

On my journey, I've experienced many things in life. It was often in the most difficult of circumstances that life's meaning became clearer. In fact, that is how this book came to be. At a very challenging point in my life, I felt called to write this book to help others better understand their life experiences.

I encourage you to join me on a guided tour through this simple book with an open mind as we explore life's journey. This book is not meant to be a step-by-step instruction manual. It is intended to be a guide for understanding and appreciating our journey. My desire is that you will find peace and acceptance in who you are and where you've been. My hope is that you will gain a fresh perspective of where you are currently. My prayer is that you will find hope and encouragement to embrace the journey ahead. My journey with God has been blessed with gifts of insight, grace and gratitude; may your journey be the same.

AS WE BEGIN OUR JOURNEY TOGETHER

O ur journey with God begins as all journeys do: *In the beginning.* These first three words, from the creation account in the Bible, provide us with a very distinctive beginning to humankind's journey.

> *Then God said: Let us make human beings in our image,*
> *after our likeness.*   *Genesis 1:26*

This verse prompts several important questions: Who is God? What does this mean that we are made in *"our image, after our likeness"?* How do our earthly beginnings in each of our families of origin affect us?

We will explore these and many other questions. As we do, I encourage you to contemplate what your life's journey is about. Obviously, the title of the book gives away the conclusion that I have come to: God has a major role in our life's journey. When talking about God we need to acknowledge that theology, which is the study of God, and its accompanying mysteries need to be considered.

It is in this context that *Our Journey WITH God* is written. Each of the four words of the book's title makes up a main section of the book. I introduced the **Our** section above, pointing out that our journey began with God. We need to understand where we have come from, and how our origin and experiences along the way affect our identity, as well as our past, present and future lives.

The second section, **Journey**, looks at our path through life to the present and beyond. In particular, we will examine the relational aspects of life's journey. We don't journey through life alone. Relationships greatly influence us throughout our journey. It then stands to reason that a relationship with God might impact us as well. The question is, can we know God, or is God some sort of abstract concept? My premise is that God is knowable. More importantly, he wants you to know him and he wants you to knowingly journey with him!

The third section of the book explores our relationship with God as we intentionally journey **WITH** him. How can we know that we are on the right path? We need a guide. As we seek to orient our lives toward God, he teaches us to trust his guidance as we become more intimate with him.

This leads us to the last section of the book, **God**. When we embrace the journey with God, we begin to see his purpose for us and our journey with him becomes clearer. As we gain a deeper understanding of who God is, we appreciate that our stories are a part of his bigger story.

At various points along the way you'll be prompted to stop and reflect on your journey. The purpose of these reflections is to draw insights from your experiences as well as provide encouragement for the journey ahead.

In the beginning was God. He has always been with us, and our journey with him never ends. Will you join me on our journey with God?

A Note from Joe

Our Journey WITH God assumes the following:

1. God exists.
2. God created.
3. God is a mystery.
4. God reveals himself to us.
5. The Bible is the primary source for our journey's exploration.

The story of creation and the journey of God's people as recounted in the Bible have profound implications for you and me on our journey through life. While you may not agree with these "assumptions," I ask that you be open to this telling of our collective human story and how it affects your personal journey. Additionally, you will find that I reference God in the masculine in order to remain true to the same voice we find in the Bible.

OUR

An Old Black and White Image

By the time Joey, our oldest son, was seven years old, he had heard for years that he was the spitting image of his dad. As an adult, I knew what people meant by this comment. Joey had no real way to fully understand and appreciate just how much he resembled me. One day I showed Joey a black and white photograph of me on my seventh birthday.

Joe circa Summer 1968

He was stunned. The look on his face was a combination of disbelief and surprise. "Who is this?" I asked Joey. "It's you...but it really looks like me," he stammered. In seeing that he looked a lot like me, Joey understood the concept of "image and likeness." Granted, it was a seven-year-old level of understanding, but that photo made quite an impact on Joey.

Joey circa Summer 1998

And the similarities didn't just end at how he looked. His personality, his energy level and his curious nature all pointed to a strong family resemblance.

Joey's unique personality and appearance are the result of a "creative" coming together of his mother and father. Those who know Maria and me, know that Joey is "our" son. In appearance, Joey is a younger version of me. Fortunately, he was blessed with Maria's angelic singing voice and not mine. These blended characteristics abound in each of our children. Sarah, our middle child, is also a blend of Maria and me. She and

I share a thrill-seeking nature that Maria definitely does not. For that reason, it was Sarah and me, not Maria—who jumped out of a perfectly good airplane from 13,000 feet. Fortunately, Sarah dances like her mom and not her "rhythm-less" dad. Our youngest, Joshua, thoughtfully considers his options before making a choice, just like Maria. Once they make decisions, they both excel at achieving their goals. Our children resemble us in many ways and their identities have been shaped accordingly. Their level of understanding and appreciation of this fact continues to grow to this day. I share these personal family anecdotes because they suggest something important and pertinent to the **Our** in *Our Journey WITH God*.

This resemblance between parent and child is rooted in God's creative design of the human person. Therefore, it is important that we understand how this came to be and what it means to us collectively and personally.

In God's Image

Then God said: Let us make human beings in our image, after our likeness.   *Genesis 1:26*

The very beginning of our existence as human beings is found in this statement. God intentionally created us to resemble himself. Humans are the only part of God's creation made in his image and likeness. This goes much deeper than Joey's identity as our child. This speaks to the very core of our identity. *Webster's Dictionary* defines identity as sameness of essential character. If you stop and think about it, this has profound implications for us as human beings. This is very personal. Our identity at the deepest level is the same as God's. The essential aspects of our being and character are the same as the God who created us. This understanding of our identity is a core, foundational aspect of our journey with him.

Now before reading further, I want to challenge you to pause and reflect on what this means to you personally. Before you do, take a look at the photo of me above. My family and I were at Kennywood, the amusement park near our home. I'm posing in my stylish 1960's mock turtleneck at a spot that encourages you to "capture the moment here." I've always remembered that day fondly—my 7th birthday—because of this photo.

At various points in this book, I will encourage you to "Capture Your Moment" with a place for reflection. I will provide prompts to stimulate your thinking. Feel free to go beyond the prompts if you desire. You can capture your thoughts in the space provided, or if you're more visual, feel free to sketch your reflections.

Capture Your Moment

Have you ever thought about being created in the image and likeness of God? How does this challenge you? How does it encourage you?

The Work of His Hands

When we moved into our current house, the back yard was an overgrown mess. One hot summer day, six-year-old Joey agreed to help me with what he called, "the war on weeds." He painted his face and put on his camouflage tee shirt and gloves and we began hacking away. To our surprise we found a treasure trove of flowers and ornamental shrubs along with a sandstone sidewalk that we didn't know existed. Beneath the overgrowth was a beautiful creation that someone had designed and planted. We have continued to nurture this landscape over time. Decades after the war on weeds, we still enjoy the original plantings some unknown gardener placed in our yard.

Early in the book of Genesis, the author recounts the story of how God created all things. We might imagine God as the original gardener. The poetic first chapter of Genesis paints a beautiful picture of the beginning. We can't know exactly how it happened, but we see the imprint of the creator all around us if we are willing to look. As our yard demonstrates, there is a foundation upon which our landscaping is woven. At the same time, it exists to be cared for and appreciated by us. The physical creation of our world also had a purpose. The second chapter of Genesis provides us with a more detailed understanding of that purpose, as God's masterpiece, created in his image and likeness, is placed in his garden.

> *Then the LORD God formed a man from the dust of the ground and breathed into his nostrils the breath of life, and the man became a living being. The LORD God planted a garden toward the east, in Eden; and there He placed the man whom He had formed.*   *Genesis 2:7-8*

In another part of the Bible the prophet Isaiah provides us with an additional image of God as our creator:

Yet you, LORD, are our Father. We are the clay, you are the potter; we are all the work of your hand.
Isaiah 64:8

This idea of God as Potter provides us with an intimate image of his involvement in our coming into being.

God, our potter, lovingly created us as his "pottery." Each created piece is made from the same raw material. Imagine yourself as a lump of clay that God placed on his wheel and masterfully spun into existence.

While watching our favorite *HGTV* show, Maria and I were mesmerized by a skilled potter at work. He made a beautiful custom set of dishes and then stamped his name into the damp clay. We, as God's masterpiece—created in his image and likeness—have been "stamped" with more than his name. We are all created with God's essential character, his identity. This core concept of identity impacts every aspect of our lives. This is true even when we don't fully understand it. We need to continually grow in our understanding of what it means to be created in God's image and likeness.

The Same and Yet Unique

In the photos of Joey and me, there is a clear resemblance between two people. Joey looks like me, but we are not the same person. The potter's set of dishes helps us to understand the significance of this. While created from the same material, each piece of the set is different from the others just as each of God's created pieces—each person—is unique.

Here at this early stage of *Our Journey WITH God*, we've looked at the foundational characteristics of what it means to be created in God's image and likeness. We've also established that as God's created beings, we are the same and yet unique. At this point it is natural to ask and expect answers as to what other characteristics we share with God our creator.

The Characteristic of Us

Image and likeness suggest that we were intentionally created to "look" and "act" like our creator. Obviously, that means we need to understand what our creator looks like and how he acts. In Genesis 1:26, we find a clue in the smallest of words, "us."

Who is "us"? In the definition of the word "us," we find a clue to help us understand this. Us is plural. Simply put, God is not an individual. God is more than one person. God is community. God belongs—as do we! Later in this book we will explore in greater depth what it means that God is community.

From the beginning, we are meant to belong. At our core as human beings we have a need to be a part of "us" in some form or another. Belonging is an important foundational part of our identity. The "us" emphasizes the fact that this need to belong was placed in us by design. Let's return to the biblical version of creation to understand this more clearly.

> *The LORD God said: It is not good for the man to be alone.*
> *I will make a helper suited to him.*
> *That is why a man leaves his father and mother and clings to his wife, and the two of them become one body.*
> *Genesis 2:18, 24*

God, knowing that living in communion is essential to his nature, created family. The story of Adam and Eve in Genesis provides us with the origin of marriage and family.

Our Family's Origin

On a nearly perfect, beautiful June day in 1986, our family began when Maria and I said, "I do." Over thirty years later, the photographs of our wedding day still make me smile warmly. Much has happened in that time. Maria and I have journeyed together through the ups and downs and twists and turns of family life. There have been times of joy and happiness as well as sadness and suffering. The most wonderful part of that journey for us were the births of our children, Joey, Sarah and Joshua.

They, each in their own unique ways, have characteristics that identify them as members of our family. As they have matured, they have also grown in their understanding of their identity and their belonging to our family. Maria's and my enthusiastic attendance and participation at countless soccer games, dance recitals and band and musical performances were ways we demonstrated our love. Our children knew they belonged to a loving family. It is a joy to experience each of their unique, ongoing journeys through life.

Many of us have seen photographs, have listened to stories or have watched videos that remind us of who we are and where we came from. We identify with those images because they help us to understand our beginnings.

Broken Family

Just how much does our family of origin affect how we identify with God? Of course, it's different for everyone, and the factors affecting our identification with God are countless. It must be acknowledged that many of us do not experience family life in a very positive way. Many people are scarred by painful experiences of abuse. Sadly, some of us have little or no sense of belonging, let alone love, with our families. Wounds are also inflicted by others in our extended families and beyond. Whatever our family history, our experiences greatly impact our perceptions of God and how we understand our own identity.

God's creation, his pottery, is often cracked and broken, as families and caregivers are not always able to function effectively in their purpose of lovingly raising children. The more wounds we experience in our upbringing and throughout our lives, the more challenging it can be for us to imagine God as loving and merciful. And to some degree, this brokenness is inherent in us all. No family is perfect, and there are very distinct and profound reasons as to why.

Capture Your Moment

What is your sense of belonging to your family of origin?
Where do you feel you belong? What does it mean to you that
you can belong to God?

The Truth of the Matter

Family life, by God's nature and design, was perfect. God was
present with Adam and Eve in his garden. They lived together
in communion with one another. This life that God had given to
his family was in essence perfect. So, what went wrong? The
answer again can be found in Genesis. In God's first words to
Adam, we find more of what it means to be created in his image
and likeness. We also find a clue as to where the break in God's
"pottery" first occurred.

*The LORD God gave the man this order: You are free
to eat from any of the trees of the garden except the
tree of knowledge of good and evil. From that tree*

you shall not eat; when you eat from it you shall die.
Genesis 2:16-17

Within these words from God, we find some of the most profound core truths of our existence.

TRUTH #1: GOD GAVE US FREEDOM TO CHOOSE
God created us with the freedom to choose. *"You are free..."* These words to Adam demonstrate God's desire for his children to freely choose. This freedom to choose is the God-given ability to exercise our free will; everything begins with this freedom.

TRUTH #2: GOOD AND EVIL EXIST
God has established for us that there is good and evil. God commands Adam to not eat from *"the tree of knowledge of good and evil."* We need to know the difference between good and evil.

TRUTH #3: GOD DESIRES THAT WE OBEY HIS COMMANDS
God commands us to not choose evil. God clearly states his command to Adam, *"...you shall not eat"*. We need to obey God by choosing what is good.

TRUTH #4: OUR CHOICES HAVE CONSEQUENCES
God is clear that our choices result in consequences, good and bad. God clearly defines for Adam the consequence of disobedience: *"you shall die."* We will experience the consequences of our actions.

These four truths impact every aspect of our existence. As we journey through life, we will continually have the opportunity to exercise our free will, to discern the difference between good and evil, to obey God's commands, and to live with the natural consequences of our choices. Our understanding and application of these truths are integral to our journey with God.

Loving Freedom

God placed Adam and Eve in the garden and gave them abundant life. They walked in his presence, content that their every need would be fulfilled. This idyllic lifestyle came with the freedom to partake of nearly everything in the garden. They lived freely in God's presence. In order to remain free, Adam and Eve needed to choose to obey God. In other words, this freedom came with limitations. It wasn't the freedom to do whatever they wanted. Just as parents set boundaries for their growing children, God defined the limits of their freedom.

It seemed like a perfect plan—except that free will opens the door to choosing to disobey God. Why would God allow us to choose if our choices might end in death? In a word, the answer is love. I'm not sure I understood the true reason behind God's decision to do this until I became a father. Witnessing a child's willful behavior gives us a glimpse into God the Father's incredible decision to allow us to choose. Only a God who embodies unconditional, unlimited love could allow his creation to freely choose to reject him over and over. This is where we understand why God would risk our disobedience and rejection. He could have created us to automatically love and obey him. However, God gives us the ability to choose because he wants us to choose him, out of love.

Capture Your Moment

How did you experience love in your family of origin? God lovingly created us; he desires that we freely choose to identify with him and belong to his family. How does this kind of love impact you?

God's Truths in Action

Good parents work hard at creating healthy boundaries that are meant to protect their children from harm. They do so out of love. One of the most challenging things for a parent is to watch their children choose to disobey. There were times when I said to our young children, "Do it because I said so." In all honesty, I simply wanted to "coerce" them to obey because it was easier for me. But healthy development in children includes a process of them exerting their own will, making their own choices between good and evil, and then learning to live with the natural consequences of their actions. Eventually, I realized that my children needed to learn to choose for themselves, and I needed to let them do so. For me, this was an example of God's truths in action.

While our experiences with all three of our children were different because of their unique personalities, God's truths still applied. Getting little Sarah to bed was downright maddening at times. Being a night owl, she wasn't always ready to go to bed when we wanted her to go. She exerted her surprisingly strong will by climbing out of bed over and over. Joey, our rule-breaking first-born, tested our patience. It seemed like the fastest way to get Joey to do something was to tell him not to do it. "Joey, you need to wear your helmet when you go out on your bike!" Guess what? It wasn't a question of if he would take the helmet off—it was when. He made unsafe choices in direct disobedience on numerous occasions. Maria and I frequently reminisce about the infamous napkin throwing incident by young Joshua during dinner. As a four-year-old, he threw his napkin on the floor and then he decided to take a stand and not pick it up.

In their own unique ways, children exert their will. They choose for themselves instead of always obeying the rules set forth by their wiser and more mature parents. In each instance, loving parents decide the appropriate consequences for their children's willful disobedience. In the case of Joshua's napkin, I told him he wasn't allowed to go outside and play in the leaves with Joey and Sarah until he picked it up and threw it away. For a period of time Josh chose to accept the consequence of not having fun with his siblings. Eventually, Josh chose to obey. These examples of childish behaviors demonstrate to a relative degree how we exert our free will, choose between wrong and right (evil and good) and that there are consequences of our choices.

This parent-child dynamic has played out since the Garden of Eden. God's truths are clear and immutable, but he does not force them upon us; he allows us to choose to accept and obey them. This raises a question that begs an answer. Why did God's children choose to disobey?

The Beginning of Disobedience

Returning to the biblical story of the Garden of Eden, we gain insight through the dialogue between Eve and the serpent. The entrance of this new character in the garden scene introduces the personification of evil. The "evil" serpent has a critical role in humanity's disobedience to God's commands. Eve is present in the garden when the crafty serpent asks her a question.

Did God really say, "You shall not eat from any of the trees in the garden?"   *Genesis 3:1*

Right from the start, the serpent seeks to create doubt: "*Did God really say...*" Initially the serpent focuses Eve's attention on the meaning of God's words. The serpent's doubt-inducing question paves the way for his next tactic. He attacks God's truth with a lie.

You certainly will not die! God knows well that when you eat of it your eyes will be opened and you will be like gods, who know good and evil.   *Genesis 3:4-5*

The serpent, by his deception, seeks to create doubt in Eve's mind about God's commandment. He does so by first denying God's truth about the consequence of disobedience. "*You certainly will not die!*" The serpent then brings God's intentions and wisdom into question. "*God knows well...*" While there is some truth in this statement—Adam and Eve did come to know good and evil—the serpent twists the truth for his purpose. Evil has inserted itself between God and his children. It does so by creating doubt about God and his truths and thus God's actual character and intentions.

Once the seeds of doubt were planted, Eve had to choose God or the serpent, good or evil. The serpent had masterfully deceived both Eve and Adam. He did so by tempting them to choose selfishly.

The woman saw that the tree was good for food and pleasing to the eyes, and the tree was desirable for gaining wisdom. So she took some of its fruit and ate it; and she also gave some to her husband, who was with her, and he ate it.   Genesis 3:6

Eve chose what was "pleasing" and "desirable" to her. In choosing self over God, she stepped over God's boundary line from good into evil. For the first time in human history, a choice was made to disobey God. Adam and Eve's disobedience is known as original sin. From that point forward humanity has struggled with conflicting desires that often seem harmless at first. However, seemingly small sin can lead to patterns of disobedience that can affect us for years.

Disobedience in Action

It surely wasn't my original sin, but I vividly remember the scene of some sinful behavior early in my life. I grew up in a housing development with an inordinate number of boys living near me. Bordered by hundred-year-old oak trees, my house had the best back yard in the neighborhood for baseball and football games. My parents' attempts at having a nice lawn didn't stand a chance against our summer WIFFLE® ball tournaments and fall football games. It was the idyllic setting for a sports-addicted adolescent.

Gathering up a bunch of guys for a game met my needs to be active, to belong and to be accepted. Yet, with all of the good, healthy fun we had, somehow it wasn't enough. One particular winter, a snowstorm had dumped six inches of perfect snowball-making snow. An epic neighborhood snowball battle ensued. At some point in the heat of battle, an errant snowball nearly struck a passing car. In that moment, a new opportunity for "fun" presented itself, and we soon found ourselves taking aim at cars heading down Meadowvale Drive. Needless to say, this was not a parentally approved activity, and any thought of it being wrong was quickly overcome by the excitement of a new challenge. Having developed a pretty good throwing arm playing all those games, I reared back and let a hard-packed snowball fly...

Sin's Beginning

The word *sin* translated from the original Hebrew text means to miss the mark or to veer off course. Both elements of this definition are important. They point back to God as the originator of a standard of behavior, the mark, and desired path or course. Missing the mark infers that there is a "targeted" behavior that should be hit. In the context of God's truths, he establishes his mark through his commands. Missing God's good targets is sin. God's desire is that we would choose his path. When we don't, we sinfully veer from his path. God allowed Adam and Eve to choose for themselves. He willingly created them, and us, with the propensity to accept or reject him and his truths. In the instant that Eve first chose to believe the serpent, all of humanity began the struggle between choosing evil over good, sin over obedience, self over God.

Back to that arching snowball. It thudded loudly onto the roof of some surely startled, unsuspecting driver. My friends and I ran for cover, nervously laughing the whole way. I quickly learned how not to get caught. I would throw the snowball with enough arch, far out in front of the moving car. This way the car would be forty or fifty yards ahead of where I was hiding. I got really good at this thrilling new "sport." I rarely missed my mark! But I had definitely veered off the path of good, clean fun with the guys.

My neighborhood experiences provided me with a wide variety of choices, good and bad. Because I was not focused on

God's truths, I often chose "bad" in order to meet my need to fit in. This need to connect and belong made me susceptible to choosing sinful behavior, which became a pattern for me as I navigated my teen years. Over time, these patterns escalated to more serious sin. While I sensed many of these behaviors were wrong, I was definitely unaware of the forces working against me.

Evil's Identity

Since Adam and Eve's first disobedient choice, humanity has been under assault by evil that seeks to turn our selfish desires away from God. The identity of an evil presence in the garden has been discussed and debated throughout history. The exact nature of the serpent can never be known. However, the personification of evil is present from the beginning to the end of the Bible. We find the evil presence with names like the devil, liar, Satan, Beelzebub, Leviathan, tempter, the prince of the demons and the great red dragon. The actual name is not important here. The existence of an evil presence is what matters. From this point forward in *Our Journey WITH God*, this evil presence will be referred to by the name of Satan.

While thinking about sin and Satan's part in it, I picked up my phone and asked, "What is the opposite of truth?" My phone answered, "Lie. A lie is a statement used intentionally for the purpose of deception." I expected that answer, but the second response was unexpected: "Falsity or falsehood is a perversion of truth originating in the deceitfulness of one party and culminating in the damage of another party." My "smart" phone had given me a surprisingly clear definition, which encapsulated who Satan is. We find him described similarly in this verse from John's Gospel:

...he is a liar and the father of lies.   *John 8:44*

Satan can also be called the father of falsity. His perversion of God's truth originated from Satan's own deceitfulness. The initiation of his falsity was Adam and Eve's disobedience, which damaged their true identity and resulted in their death. Think about it—living freely with God in their true identity gave Adam and Eve life. Choosing to pursue the false identity Satan presented brought them death.

Evil's Ways

Satan tempts us to choose something other than what God wants for us. The word temptation is rooted in the Latin word, *temptare*, which means "to feel, or try out." Satan tempts us to try out a path that appeals to our senses or feelings. Within Satan's temptation is usually a perceived notion of something better that we need to try out. He seeks to deceive us that God doesn't have our best interest at heart and that we know what's best for ourselves. Satan's deception is intended to tempt us to choose ourselves over God.

Satan tempts us to sin in order to separate us from God. When we sin, we deliberately and independently turn away from God. Our sinful behaviors, rooted in our selfish choices, affect our relationship with God. In this we see that sin is both behavioral and relational. Our sins are a departure from God's intended design in which he desires to be present with us. Inherent in God's design and truths is the ideal that we are to be "with" God as much as we are to do "what" God commands. The "what" we do in sinning has a direct impact on our relationship "with" God.

The relational impact of sin on God is clearly illustrated by a simple story. A teacher asks her young students, "What is sin?" A little boy pushes his seat back and walks up to the teacher and says, "If you are God, when I sin I'm doing this." He turns his back on the teacher, who smiles at the precocious wisdom of the little boy. As this story demonstrates, choosing to selfishly sin is choosing to turn our backs on God. Separated from him, we find it difficult to do what he commands. This cycle continues as we struggle to know who God is and who we are to be as his creation.

The Path of Separation

My childhood dream of becoming a professional baseball player ended when I didn't get picked as a walk-on in college. But, I was on the Meadowvale Drive All-Star team for hitting cars with snowballs. Temptation was very much a part of that experience. What started as an impulsive, thoughtless act, escalated into a calculated exercise of risky behavior. I knew what I was doing was wrong, but the thrill of avoiding "capture" was addictive. Plus, the accolades I got from the guys was intoxicating. Yet while I hit plenty of cars, I had begun a pattern of sinful behavior—missing the mark—as I began to make selfish choices that gave me a false sense of belonging.

My snowball throwing illustrates one instance where I had veered off onto an ungodly path—separated from God. I have chosen that path many times in life. The point is, some of my sins were a result of my giving in to unhealthy, selfish desires, while others were the result of my "giving in" to the influence of others. While I was aware of an internal struggle, I was not fully cognizant of the power of my choices. My sins led me away from God as I chose an identity and path that was not of God. This same pattern of sinful behavior exists for all of us as we journey through life.

Oh, and one last thing. If your car was hit by a snowball on Meadowvale Drive back in the mid '70's, I am truly sorry!

Capture Your Moment

Think back on your life with this concept of sin and disobedience in mind. What seemingly innocuous behaviors might have led you into greater sin? Reflect on the beginning of patterns that led you from God's path. What influenced your choices? What voices around you tempted you to choose to sin?

Pursuing the False Identity

Satan seeks to entice Adam and Eve to choose a false identity. To do so he first attacks God's identity as a truthful, sovereign God. Adam and Eve are aware of God's stated truth. Satan's initial statement suggests that God is a liar and is therefore someone other than who he says he is. If Satan's words are true, it places what Adam and Eve know about God in doubt. Satan's intention is to lure them into making a choice that he knows will separate them from God. Of their two options, Adam and Eve must decide who has the truth. If it is Satan, then God is a liar.

If it is God, then Satan is a liar. This decision between God and Satan, good and evil, is a turning point in the story of humanity. The masterpiece of God the Potter, created in God's image and likeness, chooses evil over good. In this moment, humanity's journey turns away from God in pursuit of a false identity.

Our Confused Identity

Years ago, while working as an independent consultant and trainer, I decided to hire a business coach. As she talked about my natural God-given ability to adapt to diverse people and various environments, she called me a chameleon. I reacted viscerally and negatively. She had unknowingly struck a nerve. I shared with her the story of my having been teased and ostracized by neighborhood friends. One summer as an adolescent, I connected with a new group of older kids in my neighborhood. As I hung out with them, I once again demonstrated my desire to belong by doing things I would not have typically done—just like the snowball throwing at cars. While I sensed some of the things I was doing were wrong, I enjoyed the approval that they seemed to bring. I felt accepted until one day things changed. It slowly became obvious to me that I wasn't welcome in the group anymore. Then the name calling started. I was hurt and confused by their nickname for me: The Chameleon! I was scorned and rejected, and it was devastating.

The underlying problem, of which I was unaware at the time, was that I was making choices to pursue an identity in order to "fit in" instead of choosing what was right and good based on my God-given identity. I spent years seeking the approval of others while pursuing a false identity. I am now aware that I often used my God-given "chameleon-like" abilities for the wrong reasons. I veered off course as my selfish, sinful choices kept me away from God. I believed the lies of the enemy while struggling with my identity. I sought and received worldly approval at the expense of a life with God. Many consequences have resulted from my sins, then and now. This dynamic continues for us all.

Capture Your Moment

Looking back on your life, when have you believed the lies of the enemy about your identity? Perhaps you made choices in your life for the wrong reasons. When have you sought worldly approval and pursued a false identity?

Eternal Consequences

The unfortunate consequences of choosing a false identity can be life-altering. While there are many consequences in Adam and Eve's story, two of them are particularly pertinent to our journey with God. God made the first consequence very clear to Adam. If they chose to disobey God and eat from the forbidden tree, it would result in their death. Secondly, what was not explicitly stated was that disobedience, or sin against God, could not be tolerated. Because God is pure and holy, he cannot be in the presence of sin:

> *The LORD God therefore banished him from the garden*
> *of Eden...* *Genesis 3:23*

Because of their sinful choice, Adam and Eve suffered the consequences of their actions. Once they disobeyed, everything changed for Adam and Eve. Instead of living with God in his garden, they began a journey apart from him, which ended in death.

Adam and Eve's sin also had eternal consequences that directly affect us. We have inherited Adam and Eve's sinful nature. This inheritance enslaves all of humanity in selfish sin that condemns all to death and eternal separation from God. Satan exerts his formidable will against us to deceive as many as possible in an attempt to separate us from God—*forever.* This is a reality in humanity's journey through life. Thankfully, our story doesn't end there. God is sovereign over all, including Satan, sin and death. It is possible to have the life that God intended for us. In fact, it is God's desire that we do. Our hope must be in our God, who has had a plan for us all... since the very beginning.

> *Then God said: Let us make human beings in our image,*
> *after our likeness.* *Genesis 1:26*

OUR...

By understanding our beginning as presented in the book of Genesis, we recognize several key foundational beliefs. Having been lovingly created by God, our creator, we have within us his image, which includes an innate need to belong. Just as a parent and child, we bear a profound resemblance to God. In the parent-child relationship is the essence of community, our need to belong to something loving and good. This is all a part of the perfect design of God, the Master Potter.

However, the free choice that Adam and Eve made to disobey God opened the door to an enemy who seeks to destroy God's masterpiece. From that point forward, broken, separated humanity, created in God's image and likeness, struggles with a sinful nature. Humanity continues to wander through history in search of its true identity in God. This journey continues to this day.

Where does the journey take us to next? If we knew that our creator had been seeking us all along, we could have hope, for humanity and for us as individuals. Knowing God is a critical step in our journey with God. When we move from an unknown journey to a known journey with God, everything changes. We are called to journey with God. Knowingly.

JOURNEY

The Journey to Knowing

On a recent family trip to Boston, we were frequently reminded of the early journey of the American colonists who fought for independence from Great Britain. As we came upon the narrow path marked by the red bricks of Boston's Freedom Trail, we became consciously aware of the events that occurred in each location. I thought about the people who walked this same path all those years ago. Our tour guide, dressed in period attire, brought the historic events to life as we journeyed along those cobblestone streets. The American colonists came to the new world seeking a life free from tyranny. Our history books are filled with the stories of their courageous risks and brave sacrifices.

At one point on our sightseeing journey through Boston, the red bricks of the Freedom Trail brought us to Paul Revere's house. The story of Paul Revere's "Midnight Ride" had always been one of my favorites. In the dark of night, on April 18, 1775, Revere and two other men bravely left their homes to warn the colonists that the invading British troops were on the move. The day after Revere's ride, the first shots of the American Revolution were fired, and the journey toward American Independence had begun. Something stirs within me as I wonder what it must have felt like for Revere as he galloped through the small towns outside the city of Boston shouting his warning that the British were coming! Yes, I'm a bit of a history geek, but in relating to Paul Revere and the colonists, I come to know a little more about myself. Even if you're not a history buff, there can be value in knowing our history.

Why Knowing Matters

I will never forget the moment Sarah knew beyond a doubt that she could read. We were laying side by side across her bed reading her illustrated children's Bible. Leaning on our elbows, knees bent with our feet in the air, we entered into the stories I held in my hands. Up to this point, five-year-old Sarah had been reading individual words. Joey, who is two years older than Sarah, was reading quite proficiently, and she longed to read like her big brother. It wasn't for lack of effort, as Sarah had been trying for some time, but it hadn't yet clicked for her. With my encouragement, she continued to read word by word until something changed. I remember it vividly. We turned the page to the story of Moses and the burning bush. At that moment, Sarah began to string the words together into sentences. Our excitement grew as each word flowed from her mouth. As we read about Moses coming to know God, Sarah was reading! *And she knew it!* She continued reading for a while until her excitement eventually overcame her and we jumped off the bed and ran, children's Bible in hand, to share the good news with Maria and Joey.

There is a profound difference between "knowing about" and actually "knowing." Even at her young age, Sarah knew about what it meant to read because she had observed her brother and had experienced us reading to her. But at that moment when she actually began to read, her life changed. She now knew with certainty what it meant to read.

The theme for this section of the book focuses on the word journey, but with the added dimension of knowing. A journey is not just about moving from point A to point B. It entails preparation, decisions, detours, struggles and accomplishments. All of these facets of taking a journey can be summed up in one word: knowing. And *Our Journey WITH God* is specifically about KNOWING God as we journey through life. I understand that writing in CAPS is like shouting in our social media world. However, I wrote this way to intentionally convey, beyond the shadow of a doubt, that knowing God is the great theme of life. That is why knowing God, our Creator, the Potter who formed each of us in his image, is the primary thrust for this section of the book.

One way children begin knowing about God is through the stories in the Bible. Just as Sarah progressed through the learning process of reading, we also progress in our understanding of God. We gain an appreciation for God's identity as we learn about his greater story for all of humanity. Eventually, we see how the stories of our lives are connected to those in God's stories. That is why "story" is so important to our journey.

I Know That Story

The five basic elements of every story include: setting, character, conflict, plot and theme. Even the simple story of Sarah's knowing she could read contains each element. The **setting** is right out of a Norman Rockwell painting: father and daughter together in a special place. Sarah is our main **character** and heroine. She is **conflict**ed because she is only able to read individual words. Being an independent child, she is desperately trying to master this new skill. With the introduction of a brother who is reading at a much higher level, the **plot** thickens. With the turn of a page to an illustration of Moses and a burning bush the penultimate moment arrives... Cue the dramatic music that builds as words become sentences. Finally, the victory of a life changing achievement! The **theme** is "knowing." In reading this story, you know something significant about Sarah's childhood. But unless you have met her personally, you don't really *know* Sarah.

Similarly, in the story of our journey through Boston, we only knew about the story's characters, the American colonists. We could not know personally those who had journeyed along the Freedom Trail over 200 years earlier. However, knowing about them and how their lives affected our lives as Americans is important because our life's journey as Americans is interwoven with theirs. When we relate to our country's history, that connection brings some level of meaning and understanding to us. We find something significant in the theme of freedom that runs throughout the story of those who came before us. Our identity is rooted in our history. If we choose to, we can completely ignore our history. However, on life's journey, our history is important because it defines and informs our present—and it hints at our future.

My stories of Joey recognizing himself in my photograph and Sarah learning to read are two simple illustrations that define, in a small way, our family journey together. The stories of people like Paul Revere, Samuel Adams, George Washington, Betsy Ross and Benjamin Franklin inform us about our collective journey as Americans.

That is why stories are told from generation to generation. Stories matter. Knowing about the people in our stories as well as the authors of these stories matter as well. Why is this? Why do we want to know the characters of a story? Why is it so easy to root against the bad guy? What is the reason for wanting to know how a story ends? Why do we hold out hope in even the direst of circumstances that the hero or heroine will succeed?

Journeying through God's Stories

The stories that capture our attention, keeping us on the edge of our seats and then bringing us to our feet, exultant at the redemptive climax, are similar to God's story for us, which began where he walked in his garden with his creation. Knowing this brings a particular perspective to our beginning, especially as it helps us to appreciate our identity in the way it was meant to be. The idyllic setting of that beginning gives us a deep-down desire for God's best for our lives. In the midst of living out our own "stories" we learn more about our collective journey with God. We continue to gain perspective that helps us to understand the meaning and purpose of our own unique story as it fits into God's greater story. It goes without saying that knowing how the story ends matters. But first we must know and understand the characters, setting, plot, conflict and theme of God's story. It is our story, too.

Therefore, let's revisit some of the events and characters who we met in the **Our** section. We will take some of what we know and apply it to the theme of this section to gain a deeper understanding of the meaning of the story of creation.

In the beginning, God, the Author of all things, created humans in his image and likeness. The setting for this most important of stories is a beautiful, bountiful garden. The story continues as God's primary characters, Adam and Eve, are introduced. Initially, the plot is "good," as our characters live in harmony with God. Then a new, evil character enters the story, and the first great conflict plays out.

The first story of Adam and Eve in Genesis sets the stage for the scriptural stories that follow. It also provides us with context for why we need to know and understand the stories of God and his people. As we journey through God's stories, we must always keep in mind that even though we are created in his image and likeness, a separation caused by sin still exists between God and us. When we learn about the characters in God's stories, and how they came to know him on their journey, we gain a greater understanding of what it means for us to know and journey with God.

Abram Begins a Journey with God

One of the earliest and best-known journeys in the Old Testament is that of Abram. God initiated a relationship with Abram by telling him to set out on an adventurous journey that ultimately gave birth to a great nation. God told Abram to pack up all of his belongings and leave his homeland.

> *The LORD said to Abram: Go forth from your land, your relatives, and from your father's house to a land that I will show you. I will make of you a great nation, and I will bless you; I will make your name great, so that you will be a blessing.*   *Genesis 12:1-2*

Even today, a relocation requires significant planning and commitment. It can be especially challenging when there is uncertainty about the destination. This was true in the case of Abram as well as the early American settlers. They both embarked on a journey into the unknown. Imagine packing up everything you own and moving—without a clear destination! That would be incredibly challenging, right?

Understanding the reason for their relocation helps us to appreciate why they would have taken such a leap of faith. The colonists settled in America for the promise of freedom. God's promise inspired Abram to choose to leave his home. Abram did not know it at the time, but his journey was intertwined with Adam and Eve's. Their relocation from the garden was necessitated by their poor choice. Humanity was "relocated" away from God's presence. This separation from God, caused by Adam and Eve's disobedient original sin, necessitated a renewed action by God. In Abram's journey, we see God's plan to begin anew.

God Begins Again

God, having introduced himself to Abram, then established the context of his relationship with Abram.

> *When Abram was ninety-nine years old, the LORD appeared to Abram and said: I am God the Almighty. Walk in my presence and be blameless. Between you and me I will establish my covenant, and I will multiply you exceedingly.* Genesis 17:1-2

Note the profound similarities in God's relationship with Abram and the one God shared with Adam and Eve prior to their original sin. I will paraphrase God's words to Abram in order to demonstrate God's consistent plan for humanity. In his appearance to Abram, God initiates the relationship. He does so by clearly revealing his own identity: *"I am God the Almighty."* God then expresses his desire for Abram to belong to him: *"Walk in my presence..."* Next, God points out the need for Abram to be obedient to him: *"...be blameless."* Finally, God promises the consequence of their relationship: *"I will multiply you exceedingly."*

We see God's four truths implicitly and explicitly in his words to Abram. God has provided him with the opportunity to respond to the invitation. Truth #1: Abram had the **freedom to choose** to embark on a journey with God. Truth #2: It is implied that choosing between **good and evil** is an option. Truth #3: God asks Abram to **obey** him. Truth #4: The **consequence** of Abram's "good" choice will result in a fruitful life.

These recurring truths define humanity's existence. Think about the ramifications of not living in God's truth. History is filled with the disastrous results of humankind choosing self over God. Remember that the consequences of Adam and Eve choosing evil were death and eternal separation from God. Since all of humanity has inherited this sinful nature, we are all condemned to eternal separation from God. In God's relationship with Abram we see the beginning of God's provision for humanity to return to him. Abram is overwhelmed by God's pronouncement of his role in God's plan. Abram also finds out that his role is defined by a surprising new name.

> *Abram fell face down and God said to him: For my part, here is my covenant with you: you are to become the father of a multitude of nations. No longer will you be called Abram; your name will be Abraham, for I am making you the father of a multitude of nations.*
>
> *Genesis 17:3-5*

The Kids' Nicknames

Names are important. Choosing a name for a child can be a very challenging process for parents. I remember the conversations Maria and I had during her pregnancies. We consulted name books and discussed our family names in an effort to come to a decision. We also received plenty of suggestions from well-meaning family and friends. Eventually we agreed on each child's chosen name.

At some point early in their childhood, I gave each one of our kids a nickname. Each nickname reflected their unique identity in my eyes. It was a way for me to express my love for them as individuals. I described Joey's boundless energy and enthusiasm earlier. His eyes lit up and his big, toothy grin appeared when I called him by his nickname, Sparky. Sarah had such a sweet way about her that just made me want to be with her, so I nicknamed my little girl Sweetie. Joshua loved everything about sports even before he could speak. His first word was not "mama" or "dada," but "ball." Joshua's nickname was obvious for me: Sport. Sparky, Sweetie and Sport have all outgrown their nicknames. However, I still recognize the unique identity that their names defined. And they know of my love for them, which is what matters the most.

God's Name for Us

Abraham is just one of many whose names were given or changed by God in the Bible. These names often marked important moments in the lives of those who came to know God as Abram did. Abraham's wife Sarai was renamed as Sarah. God does the same with you and me. Coming to know God personally brings each of us to a new sense of being and identity in him. While we might not know his name for us, we can know how much God cares for us. God has demonstrated throughout history that he loves his people. In fact, we can look in the Bible and recognize that one name he might call us is Beloved. Just as in my nicknames for Joey, Sarah and Joshua express my love for them, God expresses how he feels for his Beloved.

God knows us as he created us to be—not as we see ourselves, nor as the world sees us. If we acknowledge that we are God's creation, we must trust he knows each of us better than we know ourselves. While we share God's identity, we must also know that we are created uniquely. One of Maria's most treasured mementos from her deceased father is a framed quote that he gave to her and her siblings. It says, "You are an unrepeatable onceness." Its defining message is clear! Written in her dad's own handwriting, it expressed his deep acceptance, appreciation and love for her. Knowing that he felt that way about her has always inspired Maria, especially since her dad wasn't an overly effusive person. These connections between parent and child can be powerful.

As parents, we have many vivid memories of these connections. Years ago, while walking back to the car with young Joshua after a T-ball game, I reached down and tussled his mop of sweaty blond hair. I said, "Good game, Sport!" He said, "Daddy,

I know why you did that. It's because you love me." My response caught in my throat as I teared up, "Yes, that is exactly why I did that." God feels the same way about you and me. Although Joshua's nickname was important to him, it was the meaning and message the name expressed that truly mattered. As God's children, we can know the love and acceptance he has for us and for who we are in our core, created identity. It is this message of his love that God wants us to know and experience. As we will learn, he will go to any length for us to know, accept and embrace his love.

Capture Your Moment

Have you ever felt affirmed for who you are? If so, by whom? No matter your answer, what would it mean to know that God affirms you for who you are?

Abram, a Father of Many Nations

God initiated an intimate relationship with Abram. Once Abram responded to God, he gave him a new name that acknowledged his identity and pointed to Abraham's destiny. God's names for his children often point to a future and a purpose. In the case of Abram's new name, Abraham, which means the "father of many nations," it pointed to an unlikely future. Abraham surely had no idea just how significant his role was in God's plan for the redemption of God's people.

We can look back and see how God's plans unfolded for Abraham's journey, but it is much more challenging to recognize and accept God's plans while we are in the midst of them. This is especially true when our circumstances and common sense point to something very different.

This was the case for Abraham and his wife Sarah. Because they had not been able to have children, Abraham doubted that he would ever have a family, let alone be the father of a great nation. Because of their age and infertility, Abraham understandably questioned God about an heir. God's answer was a follow-up to his original promise:

...your wife Sarah is to bear you a son, and you shall call him Isaac. It is with him that I will maintain my covenant as an everlasting covenant and with his descendants after him. Genesis 17:19

God delivered on his promise as the long-awaited son, Isaac, was born. The birth of Isaac began the family lineage of Abraham that became the nation of Israel. Abraham learned to trust in God and to believe in his promises. Keeping the bigger picture of Abraham's journey in mind, we also see the more intimate story of God's involvement in Abraham's family life.

We can learn a great deal through the life lessons of God's people in the Bible. We are like an audience member with a front row seat to God's plans as they unfold throughout history.

What a Performance

One of the many blessings I experienced as a father was to see our children perform on stage in their high school musicals. Because our school is small with graduation classes under 100 students, our children were encouraged to participate in middle school instead of waiting until they were in ninth or tenth grade. By the time they were juniors and seniors, they had five years of experience and were fortunate enough to take on significant roles in the annual production. After auditioning, they were cast into appropriate roles, and I watched from a distance as they worked diligently to take on the "identity" of their characters. Even though each was "performing" a role, their uniqueness was on display for all to see.

Joey passionately performed the intense role of Judas in *Jesus Christ Superstar*. Sarah demonstrated her diverse talents as a singer and dancer in roles ranging from a Munchkin in the *Wizard of Oz* to a love-struck teen in *Bye Bye Birdie* to a demon in *Superstar*. Sixteen-year-old Joshua, with his surprisingly full beard, sincerely commanded the stage as the humble Tevye in *Fiddler on the Roof.*

These young actors and actresses transcended their everyday identity and took on their roles in the larger cast. We would marvel each year at how they could make us laugh and cry as we saw the auditorium stage transformed into a different era and place. Just as any good story does, each of the musicals brought a storyline filled with plot twists and conflicts that ultimately led to a thematic conclusion that brought the audience to their feet.

The same is true for Abraham and his descendants in God's "production" of how he brings his people back to himself. Understanding the setting, we meet the cast, learn the plot and witness the conflict. As we come to know the cast, we eventually come away from the story understanding the theme, or in the case of God's story, the message he wants us to know. That message is that God loves us, and he wants us to know him and to journey with him.

Join me as we journey through God's dramatic love story, beginning with Abraham. We will see the plot thicken and the conflict deepen as the "cast" of Abraham's descendants struggle with the same issues we saw Adam and Eve experience in the Garden of Eden.

Imagine yourself entering a beautiful auditorium for the performance of *Abraham's Family Journey with God*. The usher hands you a playbill as she leads you to your seat. As you settle into your seat, you open the playbill to learn about the production. One of the first things you come across is a note from the director that I have taken the literary license to write from God's perspective.

Abraham's Family Journey with God
A Divine Performance

Director's Note

A willingness to travel to an unknown place initiates a journey. From the time that I created Adam and Eve and lovingly placed them in my garden, my desire was for them to live in my presence. I gave them the ability to freely choose me and my truths out of love. Unfortunately, they chose selfishly. Therefore, being true to myself, I had to send them away from my presence. Abraham's Family Journey with God tells the story of how I brought humanity back to me.

Like many of the stories you have heard, Abraham's family story is My Story. It is a story of love, obedience and trust. It is a story of making choices that lead to blessings, trials and even bondage. Ultimately, it is a love story that leads to deliverance and redemption.

Performers in any great production have experienced the influence of their Director. Through many hours of toil and hard work, actors and actresses have taken direction to better perform their roles. As the Creator and Director, I know what each performer is capable of and I challenge them to find their best within them. Once the curtain opens and they step in front of the audience, they are no longer thinking about all of the rehearsals and practices. They have become who I directed them to be, as they perform their roles for the audience. While I am not physically on stage with them during the performance, they sense my presence. They know my desire is for them to be their best and for each individual to deliver their role as a part of the larger cast.

It is my hope that in the story of Abraham and his family, you will see some part of yourself. I hope you can experience Abraham's Family Journey with God with an open mind and a willing heart. I want you to know that my greatest desire is for you to know me and my love for you, so that you might choose to journey with me.

Love,

God, your Father

CAST	NAME MEANING
Abraham	Father of Many Nations
Isaac	Laughter
Jacob/Israel	Replace/Wrestles with God
12 Sons	The Twelve Tribes of Israel
Joseph	May God Add

Scene List

Act I: Abraham's New Home

Isaac's Miraculous Birth .... Abraham, Sarah, Isaac

The Test of Abraham's Faith........... Abraham, Isaac, God's Angel

God's Provision ....Abraham, Isaac, Ram

Act II: The Lands of Abraham's Families

Isaac's Wife Rebekah..................Abraham's Servant, Rebekah

Twins Wrestling .... Isaac, Rebekah, Esau, Jacob

Stolen Birthright...................................... Jacob, Esau

Isaac's Family Survives a Famine..... Isaac's Family, King Abimelech

Act III: Jacob's Lands

Jacob Deceives Isaac .... Isaac, Jacob

Jacob's Wives Bear 12 Sons...............Jacob, Leah, Rachel, 12 Sons

Jacob's Wrestling Match.................... Jacob, God's Messenger

Jacob and Esau Reconcile .... Jacob, Esau

Act IV: Jacob's Family Movement

Joseph, the Favored Son.................... Jacob, Joseph, Brothers

Brothers' Betrayal .... Joseph, Brothers

Interpreter of Dreams ....Joseph, Pharaoh's Servants

Once a Slave, Now a Deliverer .... Joseph, Jacob's Family

Plot Summary

Act I

The beginning of Abraham's story finds him and his wife, Sarah, laughing at God's promise of a son in their old age. God delivers on his promise and names their son Isaac, which means "laughter." While Abraham proved his faith earlier when he obeyed God by moving from his homeland, his faith is greatly tested when God asks him to sacrifice Isaac. God honors Abraham's willingness to do so by stopping him short of killing Isaac and by providing a sacrificial ram in Isaac's place. God lives up to his promises when his children obediently follow him.

(See Genesis chapters 12 – 22 for Abraham's story)

Act II

Abraham's dying wish is for Isaac to marry a woman from Abraham's people. He sends his servant to his original home, where he finds Rebekah. Like Sarah, Rebekah is unable to conceive children until one day following Isaac's prayer, she is found with twins. A sibling rivalry begins even before the boys are born, as Rebekah feels them wrestling in her womb. The story unfolds as the younger twin, Jacob, bargains for the birthright of Esau, his older brother. Esau relinquishes it for a cup of soup. Later on, during a famine, God asks Isaac to trust him instead of going to Abimelech, King of the Philistines. Despite family strife and famine, God provides.

(See Genesis chapters 24 – 26 for Isaac's story)

Act III

In one of his many deceitful acts, Jacob deceives his blind and dying father, Isaac, to attain Esau's rightful blessing. Jacob's wives and their maidservants bear him twelve sons. Jacob then wrestles with God's angel in pursuit of God's blessing. A permanent injury to his hip leaves Jacob with a painful reminder of his stubbornness—and a new name, Israel. The journey with God provides opportunities for faithfulness and disobedience.

(See Genesis chapters 27 – 35 for Jacob's story)

Act IV

Joseph was the first born to Jacob's beloved Rachel. He becomes Jacob's favorite son, which creates jealousy among the older brothers. Joseph tells his brothers of his dream, in which he will rule over them. This prompts the brothers to plot to kill Joseph, but instead they sell him into slavery. Joseph first serves in the pharaoh's house as a servant. He then ends up being unjustly imprisoned. There, Joseph's gift of interpreting dreams proves invaluable as he interprets pharaoh's dream of a coming time of abundance and then famine. Joseph is placed in charge of all the lands of Egypt. As the famine threatens Jacob's family, his sons travel to Egypt in search of food. After testing his brothers, Joseph mercifully provides for his family, who are happily reconciled with their brother as they move to Egypt. God always delivers his people, and the journey continues...

(See Genesis chapters 37 – 50 for Joseph's story)

After the Performance

There is a palpable buzz after a live theater production. Audience members excitedly discuss their favorite scenes and revel in the outstanding individual performances and captivating ensemble numbers. After the curtain call for our high school musicals, I always rushed out into the hallway to meet the performers. I still swell with pride thinking of Joey, Sarah and Joshua walking down the hall to meet their adoring fans. To me they were still Sparky, Sweetie and Sport. Tearful hugs of joy followed as I told them how incredibly proud I was of them. Then I would step aside and watch as they met their fans. With each of our children I impressed upon them how important it was to spend time after the performance with the people, young and old, who wanted to meet and congratulate them.

Witnessing something special like a great theater performance affects us as humans. Parents having the opportunity to see the joy their children bring to others is amazing. I imagine God feeling the same way about you and me.

Capture Your Moment

When have you and/or members of your family had a profound impact on others? What would it mean to know God is looking upon you with great pride and satisfaction?

The Challenge of Journey

After reading the playbill and reflecting on *Abraham's Family Journey with God*, think about God's presence in all of history. Observing the characters in God's stories can have a profound impact on us. This is true as we experience both the highs and the lows of their lives. We can see how God has always had a plan for our redemption even in the direst of circumstances. But living through those circumstances is easier said than done. Choosing to follow God and his truths, with temptations to disobey coming from within us and from without, is one of the toughest challenges of the journey. In the Bible, many good and bad choices were made by God's people despite their knowing him. Just like performers who occasionally forget their lines or miss their cue, we may miss the mark or veer off course. Please understand that I am not suggesting that life is a performance. I use the performance analogy to provide a different perspective on how we journey with God. By looking at the lives of those who have gone before us, we can apply the lessons they learned to our own lives. However, we always need to remember that everything begins with God, who is sovereign over all.

Wandering Off

Imagine a family at the beach with toddlers wobbling around on the sand and testing their limits in the waves. As children explore, their parents remain hyper-vigilant to ensure their safety. A parent's greatest fear is that a young child will wander off and become separated.

As we got out of our cars at our parents' home one unseasonably warm December afternoon, I asked, "Where's Sarah?" "I thought she was with you!" my sister Laurie responded. Our families had been out together on our annual event to cut down our Christmas trees. Having already dropped our tree off at our house, we had just arrived at our parents' house to deliver their tree. Sarah rode in Laurie's car on the way to the tree farm and again from the tree farm back to our house. However, we had each assumed she was in the other's car as we drove from our house to our parents' home. I'll never forget the mad dash back to our house to rescue eight-year-old Sarah, who had been left behind. My mind raced during that frantic fifteen-minute drive in our bright red Jeep Grand Cherokee, and I admittedly exceeded the speed limit. Nothing was going to stop me from getting to Sarah. The relief I felt upon seeing that Sarah was safe was nearly overwhelming. Having Sarah back in our care made everything right. Imagine God as a parent desperately wanting us back in his care. What would he be willing to do to make that happen? His stories provide us with the answers.

From the time that Abraham left his homeland until the Israelites settled in God's Promised Land, they continually wandered away from God. Although the Israelites were God's chosen, beloved people, they wandered from him, both figuratively and literally. In choosing for themselves, they became separated from God and their literal wandering began. When they figuratively lost sight of him and his truths they made terribly poor choices. Giving in to the temptation to choose self over God caused their wandering away from him. God, in his infinite love and patience, continually sought to bring them back to him.

Found by God

In *Abraham's Family Journey with God*, our story ended with Jacob's family having to leave their homes and travel to Egypt in order to survive a great famine. They remained in Egypt and grew to be a large nation. Generations passed, and a new pharaoh rose to power and enslaved all of Israel.

Centuries later, another character entered God's story. Baby Moses was born in slavery, and to protect him from the murderous pharaoh, his mother set him adrift in a basket on the Nile River. Moses was found by the pharaoh's daughter and he became a member of their family. In this story, God ensured that young Moses was rescued from the river and even nursed by his own mother. Moses became a prince and lived for forty years in the house of the pharaoh. Eventually, Moses fled after rashly killing a slave-driver. He ended up in the desert, where he was rescued by a woman who became his wife. Taken into the family of her father, Jethro, Moses became a shepherd. Here, the story takes an even more fascinating turn as Moses sees something highly unusual in the mountains.

Moses Comes to Know God

The story of the conversation between God and Moses in the book of Exodus exemplifies the deeply personal experience of coming to know God. Moses' encounter with God at the burning bush is quite instructive to us on our journey with God. Let's walk through this passage to understand the progression of this personal encounter.

When the LORD saw that he had turned aside to look, God called out to him from the bush: Moses! Moses! He answered, "Here I am."　　　　　*Exodus 3:4*

Notice that it is God who initiates the meeting, just as he did with Adam, Abraham, Isaac and Jacob. God uses the burning bush to capture Moses' attention. Keep in mind that Moses is at work when this occurs. He is doing his job as a shepherd. Once Moses physically turns away from his flock, God then calls him by name.

Does Moses' response seem rather foolish? *"Here I am."* I wonder if at some point in the future Moses thought to himself, "You knucklehead! 'Here I am.' What kind of response was that?!? Of course, the Lord knew who and where I was!" But in reality, this response is profound because Moses presents himself to God. Until this moment, Moses only knows "about" God. For the first time in his life, Moses knows now that God is alive and real, and he enters into a relationship with God.

> *God said: "Do not come near! Remove your sandals from your feet, for the place where you stand is holy ground. I am the God of your father, he continued, the God of Abraham, the God of Isaac, and the God of Jacob." Moses hid his face, for he was afraid to look at God.*
>
> *Exodus 3:4-6*

The next thing God does is to explain the situation to Moses: *"...where you stand is holy ground."* God essentially tells Moses he is standing in his (God's) presence. Then God clarifies who he is. In essence he says, "I am the God you've known about your whole life." The God of his ancestors, about whom Moses had heard stories from his mother, was the same God speaking directly to him on the mountain.

Because God is the author of these stories, he refers to them to help Moses understand. Notice that God's explanation provides a sense of belonging as he includes Moses' beloved forefathers, Abraham, Isaac and Jacob. Now, Moses knows with whom he is speaking, and that knowledge drives his response. He is overcome by a profound sense of fear or reverence. He is in the presence of God. The conversation continues and Moses eventually asks God what his name is:

> *God replied to Moses: I am who I am. Then he added: This is what you will tell the Israelites: I AM has sent me to you. God spoke further to Moses: This is what you will say to the Israelites: The LORD, the God of your ancestors, the God of Abraham, the God of Isaac, and the God of Jacob, has sent me to you. This is my name forever; this is my title for all generations.*
>
> *Exodus 3:14-15*

This name that God speaks to Moses—I AM—defines God's identity at a most personal level. There is profound meaning in the name, but at its core it means "I exist." God is telling Moses that he has always existed and that he has always been present with his people. The Israelites held God's name in such great reverence that they didn't even say it out loud for fear of using it in vain. Their pronunciation of the word in Hebrew, YHWH, sounds like "Yahweh." When we see the name in the English translations of the Old Testament, we see it written in small caps lettering as the word LORD. It appears this way in the Old Testament nearly 7,000 times. As we have seen, names are very significant in the Bible, none more so than God's.

For Moses, everything that has happened begins to make sense to him in a way he couldn't have understood before he met God. Moses now knows God personally, and he understands that he is a child of God. Because Moses knows God's true identity, YHWH, Moses begins to understand his own identity in a new way. This understanding also emphasizes Moses' sense of belonging to God's people enslaved in Egypt. These realizations are incomplete, but something profound has changed in Moses. Most importantly, Moses is in a knowing relationship with God. Once that relationship has been established, God points Moses in a new direction.

As the conversation continues, Moses resists God's suggestion to confront the pharaoh and to serve as God's instrument to deliver his people from bondage. Ultimately, God brings Moses to the understanding that he is going to journey with him back to Egypt to free the Israelites. Moses has journeyed for the first eighty years of his life knowing "about" God. Up to this point he has identified as an Israelite, as an Egyptian, and as a Midianite by marriage. Moses belonged to these people in varying ways. All that Moses has experienced throughout his life, good and bad, defines who he has been. But it does not establish his true identity nor determine his destiny.

Now as a knowing member of God's family, Moses continues his journey in relationship with God. Because it is his primal, essential relationship, Moses' new identity as a child in God's family takes precedence over all others.

There are several changes that occur in Moses as he comes to know God:

1. He gains a new understanding of his identity and a sense of belonging to God.
2. This understanding results in Moses willingly embarking on a new journey with God.
3. He accepts his unique role in God's plan.

Imagine taking a job that required you to confront the most powerful man in the world...with nothing but a shepherd's staff! At the burning bush, Moses accepted his role as God's deliverer. Despite the doubts that he expressed to God, he willingly trusted God. God's assurance that he would be with Moses as he stepped forward in faith is the next great "Act" in Moses' role in life. But now he does so with God as his Director. In his new role, Moses embraces his true identity as God's instrument to deliver the Israelites from slavery.

Why is Moses' story so important to our journey? Like Moses, we can find our true identity in a personal relationship with God, our loving Father. We then realize that we belong to God and his family. Understanding our true identity and sense of belonging allows us to embark on a new journey with God. It is on our journey with God that he reveals his plans for our unique role. (We will explore this concept of our unique role in God's plan later in *Our Journey WITH God*.)

Capture Your Moment

Who and what have you been afraid to confront in your life?
How would a greater understanding of who God is in your life
impact your identity and destiny?

The Deliverers

Moses' place in the history of Israel is unique. Like Joseph before him, Moses experienced many trials and challenges in becoming God's instrument to deliver his people. Despised by his brothers and sold into bondage, Joseph became their deliverer from starvation. Four hundred years later Moses, who was raised in the pharaoh's house, confronted the pharaoh himself as God's deliverer of the Israelites from the bondage of slavery. Joseph's and Moses' lives foreshadowed the coming of the ultimate deliverer for God's people.

Centuries after Moses' time, Israel was living under the rule of the Roman Empire. In God's chosen time, he sent his angel Gabriel to Mary, a young Jewish girl. Mary, a virgin betrothed to the carpenter Joseph, accepted the news from Gabriel that she was pregnant with God's Son. After hearing from Gabriel that Mary's pregnancy was of God, Joseph married her. Jesus was born in a simple stable, and he grew up in relative obscurity. Thirty years later, Jesus became a threat to the ruling class in Israel and was brutally tortured and suffered an excruciating death on a cross. The story of Jesus' life, death and resurrection is the most important story of all time. Jesus, the ultimate deliverer, was sacrificed to free God's people from the bondage of sin and death. From the time Adam and Eve walked out of the garden, humankind was lost and in need of finding God. In Jesus, God provided a way back to himself, once and for all.

Where All Journeys Intersect

On my journey with God, I worked for ten years as a religious education director. There were times when I had to occasionally fill in at the last minute for an unexpectedly absent teacher. With no time for preparation, I relied on my "timeline" message to teach the lesson. I would review the scheduled lesson, then figure out where it fit on God's timeline of history. I would draw a line the entire length of the classroom whiteboard. On the left end of the line I typically drew a tree to depict creation and the Garden of Eden. I then asked the kids to tell me what their favorite Bible stories were. I drew each image they provided at the appropriate point along the timeline. We always had fun with this activity. The kids enjoyed teasing me about my stick figures and funny looking animals on Noah's ark. The image of Moses and his staff often included the tablets of the Ten Commandments. A star, high above all of the other images depicted the momentous event of Jesus' birth. If the kids didn't volunteer it, I made sure to always place Jesus' cross near the center of the timeline. Immediately after drawing the cross, I would announce that Jesus' death on the cross was the most important moment in all of history. I explained that every story on our timeline pointed to the cross in some way.

In the higher grades the kids had a greater knowledge of events, and I challenged them to think about the specifics of Jesus' words and the events in his life. Peter walking on water was a fun image to draw. The woman at the well was another significant event they often remembered. When someone contributed one of Jesus' *"I am"* statements, I would explain the meaning behind each as I drew them on the timeline. The vine was easy to draw, and my sheep were pretty good standing beside the good shepherd, but light of the world was a challenge.

At the end of my lesson I always asked the kids to draw themselves on the timeline and sign their names. No matter their age, their eagerness to do so demonstrated to me that they desired to be a part of God's story.

The timeline lesson provided a great visual of the Old Testament pointing forward to the promised Messiah just as the New Testament focuses on Jesus directly. Jesus is the focal point of God's timeline in the most pivotal moment in all of history. God the Father sent his only Son to suffer and die for all sin. That is why all journeys intersect at the cross of Jesus Christ.

Jesus' Identity Revealed

Knowing the story of Jesus helps us to understand and appreciate who he was, how he lived and why he died. Jesus lived a sinless life among the Jewish people who were living under Roman rule. In his last three years, Jesus developed intimate relationships with a small group of followers. He taught them God's truths and he demonstrated God's love by caring for the sick, the poor, the crippled and the blind. In those three years, the disciples gained an understanding of who Jesus truly was.

Jesus was very clear about his own identity. This clarity both drew people toward Jesus while causing others to reject him and turn away. His notoriety increased, as many were curious to know this wise prophet. Despite his loving, caring nature and truthfulness, Jesus' presence caused disturbances among the Jewish people, particularly the religious leaders. His words and actions undermined the controlling lies of those leaders. In one intense exchange in the Gospel of John, Jesus' identity is a prominent theme.

> *So Jesus said (to them), "When you lift up the Son of Man,*
> *then you will realize that I AM, and that I do nothing*
> *on my own, but I say only what the Father taught me.*
> *The one who sent me is with me. He has not left me*
> *alone, because I always do what is pleasing to him."*
> *John 8:28-29*

Jesus revealed several aspects of his identity and purpose in this statement. First, Jesus predicted his crucifixion when he said, *"When you lift up..."* and in so doing Jesus made it clear that he would be doing the will of his Father. Second, Jesus' reference to himself as *"the Son of Man"* pointed to his humanity and his role as the prophesied Messiah. His Jewish audience, particularly the religious leaders, clearly understood Jesus' reference to their prophetic scriptures. Third, Jesus proclaimed that he is *"I AM"*. The Jews recognized this name for God because they knew well the story of Moses when God told Moses his name was I AM. In this passage, Jesus had identified himself as both human and divine.

The dialogue escalated into a debate about ancestry which prompts a response by the leaders that Abraham is their father. Jesus challenged the authenticity of their Jewish ancestry; in essence, he challenged their identity.

> *You belong to your father the devil and you willingly*
> *carry out your father's desires. He was a murderer from*
> *the beginning and does not stand in truth, because*
> *there is no truth in him. When he tells a lie, he speaks*

in character, because he is a liar and the father of lies.
John 8:44

Jesus was confronting not only their behaviors but their chosen, false identity as well. Jesus refers back to the beginning and identifies the pious Jews as belonging to the devil himself. Ouch! These words of Jesus could not have been more condemning to these followers of the Jewish laws and traditions.

In response to Jesus' characterization, they claim that Jesus is possessed. Not only does Jesus rebuke them in this, Jesus eventually brings everything back to what matters most, God his Father.

Jesus answered, "If I glorify myself, my glory is worth nothing; but it is my Father who glorifies me, of whom you say, 'He is our God.' **You do not know him, but I know him.** *And if I should say that I do not know him, I would be like you a liar. But I do know him and I keep his word."*
John 8:54-55 (Emphasis added.)

"You do not know him, but I know him." There it is! Knowing "about" God is one thing. But knowing him personally and being in relationship with him is another thing entirely. Jesus himself is the one who makes this clear.

The result of this contentious dialogue is that the religious leaders seek to physically attack and kill Jesus.

So they picked up stones to throw at him; but Jesus hid and went out of the temple area. *John 8:59*

Jesus adeptly handled each and every interaction with the Jewish people and their leaders. In doing so Jesus frequently demonstrated just how far they had wandered from the God of their fathers. Nothing caused more consternation than Jesus' claim that he was God's Son. This was more than the religious leaders could bear, and it ultimately sealed Jesus' fate. They knew they had to eliminate Jesus or lose control of their followers. In one eventful week, beginning with his triumphal entrance into Jerusalem, Jesus was eventually arrested and brought to trial.

> *When it was morning, all the chief priests and the elders*
> *of the people took counsel against Jesus to put him to*
> *death. They bound him, led him away, and handed him*
> *over to Pilate, the governor.*   Matthew 27:1-2

As he stood in the midst of the crowd shouting, "Crucify him!" Jesus knew he was going to suffer and die for the same people demanding his death. He silently received the mocking and an incredibly painful crown of thorns from the Roman guards. He willingly chose to die for their sins as well. Because he could find no guilt in Jesus, Pontius Pilate tried to assuage the crowds with a violent and bloody scourging. Jesus willingly died for Pilate and the men who beat him, too. As he stumbled and fell under the weight of the cross he was forced to carry, Jesus knew that he was being sacrificed for the sins of those who jeered him.

Jesus' Purpose

As a Jew, Jesus was intimately aware of the system of sacrifices necessary for the atonement of sin. We read in the book of Leviticus that this system was instituted by God. It required that various animal sacrifices be made as atonement for sin. The people would bring their animal sacrifice to the temple in order to be reconciled with God. The actual temple in Jerusalem was built in order to facilitate what became an intricate process that the Jewish priests administered and controlled.

My friend and I were sitting in an empty church talking about our faith. Looking up at the cross she sincerely asked me, "Why is Jesus called the Lamb of God?" I gave her my best explanation of the Jewish system of sacrifice that culminated every year on the Day of Atonement. I told her how on that day, only the high priest entered the Holiest of Holy Places behind the veil that separated the people from God's presence in the temple. There, the blood of an unblemished lamb was poured out to atone for the sins of the nation of Israel. I said, "When he died on the cross, Jesus, as God's perfect lamb, atoned for all sin...once and for all." I continued, "In the moment of Jesus' death, the temple veil separating God from his people was torn from top to bottom. Jesus had paid the price that brought us back from our separation from God. Humanity was reconciled with God through Jesus' sacrifice." As tears streamed down her cheeks, my friend understood God's loving sacrifice more clearly.

Jesus willingly chose to submit to his Father's will to be the final atoning sacrifice for sin. Hanging on the cross, Jesus uttered his last words,

"It is finished."   *John 19:30*

Jesus knew that he had atoned for the sins of all of humanity. As God's perfect, sinless, sacrificial lamb, Jesus had embraced his true identity and accepted his role as his Father's deliverer.

Capture Your Moment

What does it mean to you that Jesus died to atone for
your sins?

The Journey to Resurrection

Jesus' purpose did not end at his sacrificial last breath on
the cross. God's plan was to provide a way for humanity to
return to him.

> For the wages of sin is death, but the gift of God is
> **eternal** life in Christ Jesus our Lord.
>
> Romans 6:23 (Emphasis added.)

The "but" in the middle of this verse is perhaps the most
important "but" ever spoken because it points to the deliverer
of all of humanity from sin and death. It also points to eternal
life that results from God's gift of his Son. After his death, Jesus
was placed in a tomb and his followers scattered in fear for their
lives. Three days later, as Jesus predicted, the tomb was empty.

Jesus answered them, "Destroy this temple, and in three days I will raise it up."   *John 2:19*

Jesus spoke these words in reference to his own body, not the actual temple. It was only after Jesus rose from the dead that his followers understood that he had predicted his resurrection.

Therefore, when he was raised from the dead, his disciples remembered that he had said this, and they came to believe the scripture and the word Jesus had spoken.   *John 2:22*

Jesus' resurrection points to the ultimate destination for humanity—eternal life with God. The question we need to answer for ourselves is: do I "believe the scripture and the word Jesus had spoken"?

My Step of Faith

Having been raised in the church, I "knew about" God and had heard Jesus' words my whole life, but...

In February of 1998 my seemingly picture-perfect life was not as it appeared. Joshua, our third child, had been born six months earlier. We were excitedly fixing up our beautiful new home on a tree-lined street in an idyllic community. Having finished my MBA four years earlier, my consulting business was growing so fast I could barely keep up with the demands. Maria was enjoying her new arrangement of working full-time from home. Despite all this, deep down inside I felt empty and lost. I was on my own path in life, and unbeknownst to me, it was a dark path.

One day as I drove to the airport on my way to a business conference, I cried out in frustration that I wanted God to prove to me that he was there. I even asked for a sign. By the time I arrived at the conference I had forgotten my "prayer." Three days later on Sunday, the final day of the conference, I sat in a roomful of people listening to a woman speak about her journey to Christ. She explained in detail that without a savior we would suffer eternal separation from God. She made it clear as to what it meant to accept Jesus Christ as Savior and how we needed to embrace him as Lord of our lives as she shared this passage:

...he humbled himself, becoming obedient to death, even death on a cross. Because of this, God greatly exalted him and bestowed on him the name that is above every name, that at the name of Jesus every knee should bend, of those in heaven and on earth and under the earth, and every tongue confess that Jesus Christ is Lord, to the glory of God the Father. Philippians 2:8-11

Everything clicked in my mind, and my heart beat faster as I sensed something significant was happening to me. I had heard that Jesus was Lord but didn't completely understand how it applied to me. I realized that I no longer wanted to be on the selfish path I was traveling. I wanted Jesus to take control of my life and lead me.

At the end of her talk, a gentleman gave an invitation for people to come forward if they wanted to commit their life to Christ. It seemed that his invitation was meant for me alone. I had forgotten that three days earlier I had asked God for a sign. In that instant I noticed a clear path from where I was standing, through the crowd to the man who had made the invitation. I thought, "Is this my sign?" In a moment of doubt, I looked around to see if I knew the people standing near me. Just then I felt a tug on my shoulder and turned around to see who it was. There was no one there! That was enough of a sign for me. I stepped forward in faith to the front of the room. A small group assembled around me in support of my decision. I was led in a prayer very similar to the one I will share with you shortly. God had sought me out and I turned to him. I had accepted God's loving, sacrificial gift of life, a gift paid for by Jesus on the cross 2,000 years ago—*for me, personally.* My life has never been the same since that day when I began my knowing journey with him.

I share my story with you for several reasons. First, it is my testimony of how I came to fully embrace "God's stories and Jesus' words" about my salvation from sin. Second, everything changed at that moment. I had made a conscious decision to commit to Jesus as Lord of my life. Third, we all have a choice as to which path we will take in life. Which one have you chosen?

Jesus is the Gate

I have always found it interesting that the sign God gave me on the day I committed my life to Christ was a path. Stepping onto that path set me on my journey with God. I didn't realize it at the time, but I had chosen the narrow path.

Enter through the narrow gate; for the gate is wide and the road broad that leads to destruction, and those who enter through it are many. How narrow the gate and constricted the road that leads to life. And those who find it are few.
Matthew 7:13-14

This verse is found in the midst of the many points Jesus made in his Sermon on the Mount. In it, Jesus highlights the narrow gate that *"leads to life."* The message here? Find the path that leads to the narrow gate, because all other paths lead to destruction.

I am the gate. Whoever enters through me will be saved, and will come in and go out and find pasture. John 10:9

The path that leads to the narrow gate is the one that leads to a person, Jesus Christ. He is lovingly waiting; his scarred hands are outstretched, inviting you to step through the gate.

Will You Step Through the Gate?

Do we realize that the same God who called out to Moses from the burning bush desires that we step through the gate? Like Moses, we have the opportunity to respond, "Here I am." God has done the work to prepare the way back to him, but we have to step through his gate. While God's call probably won't come to us from a burning bush, we still have the opportunity to respond, "I want to know you, Lord, and I choose to accept your gift of salvation."

You may already know God personally. If you do, that is wonderful. You may want to recommit your life to him with the following prayer. If you want to know God personally or are not sure that you know him, here is an opportunity to ask Jesus to come into your life as Savior and Lord.

You may feel as though you're standing at an unknown gate, not sure what to do. Perhaps you've never realized that you were lost on the path of sinfulness. But your mind, your soul and your heart are hoping beyond hope that Jesus really is there. This brief prayer allows you to step through his gate for the first time or renew your journey with him.

The Journey Prayer

Having stepped through the gate, imagine that you are in God's holy presence. Feel his love for you. Let him know your love for him by praying *The Journey Prayer*. You may want to bow your head and open your hands in a gesture of surrender.

- Lord Jesus Christ, I am sorry for the times I have chosen to do wrong and wandered from you and your love. (Take a few minutes to ask Jesus' forgiveness for anything specific that is on your conscience.)
- Please forgive me for all of my sinful choices. I now turn from the path that leads me away from you.
- Thank you for dying on the cross for me so that my sins could be forgiven and my separation from you ended. I accept your gracious, sacrificial gift.
- I acknowledge you as my Savior.
- I surrender my life to you as my Lord and trust that you will be with me forever.
- In your name I pray. Amen.

If you just prayed this for the first time, trust that Jesus did in fact hear you. It is important to realize that faith is not a feeling. You may not feel any difference at all. You may experience doubt as to the reality of your experience. That is normal and why support from mature Christians is important at this point. If you don't attend church, make that your first prayer request to God. Ask him to lead you to one. It is important to engage with a church community and be guided by a pastor who can help you on your journey with God. Once you know God, you can expect that things will change: your identity, your journey and your destination. I invite you to share with me that you have taken this step. You can reach me through my website (www.joekillian.com).

Beyond the Gate

Early in my journey with Christ I found myself questioning where I was going in my life. In search of answers, I went for a hike in the woods and came upon a stream. I tossed a broken tree branch into the water. I watched it bounce through the rough spots created by larger stones in the middle of the stream. At one point it found its way into calmer waters and almost washed up onto the shore. Then it was pulled back out into the main part of the stream to continue its journey. Eventually it passed through a bend in the stream and I lost sight of it altogether. For me, the stick floating down the stream symbolizes our journey with God.

If we are the stick and God is the stream, what does it mean for us to allow him to carry us through life? God carries us through the turbulent times of life just as he does in the peaceful. We can fight against the flow, and we often do, but what happens when we accept that we are not in control? We come to embrace our journey with God and learn to trust in his loving care! We also don't know what's in store around the next bend. That's what makes our journey with God such an adventure. Life is full of surprises, good and bad. But God is always with us.

After losing sight of the branch, I sat down on a large boulder that was perched above a little eddy. I sat staring at a little pool of calm water. The water was smooth and clear and I could see the sandy bottom a foot below the surface. I absent-mindedly picked up a handful of pebbles and began dropping them into the eddy. No bigger than a fingernail, they each fluttered to the bottom and settled in the sand. At first, they formed a random pattern. As I dropped more pebbles I was surprised to see an image taking shape. Dropping the last of the pebbles I watched in amazement at the shape they formed—the rough image of a cross.

I returned home and sketched the cross of pebbles, along with my reflections about this particular journey through the woods. When I look back on the cross I sketched nearly 20 years ago, I do so with hindsight. I reflect on the challenges that I experienced that day as well as the many I have faced since then, some big, others small. But through it all I have seen God's hand at work in my life.

The cross is the most recognizable of all Christian symbols. While recognizing its beauty in many works of art, we must never forget the brutal reality that it represents. On it, Jesus died a horrific death so that the sins of all humanity could be forgiven. But what does that mean to you and me on our journey with God? When we accept Jesus' sacrifice for our own individual sins, it does come at a cost. Jesus made this clear.

Then he said to all, "If anyone wishes to come after me, he must deny himself and take up his cross daily and follow me."   *Luke 9:23*

Capture Your Moment

Journeying with God is going to be a challenge. Jesus promised it! What does this mean to you at this point on your journey?

Our Freedom Trail

Remember the Freedom Trail? The red brick path that we followed in Boston is only that, a path. We may be aware of the stories of events that happened at each of the historic sites, but awareness is not enough when it comes to relationships. Before I met her, I was aware of Maria, my sister's friend in college. I had no idea that when our paths crossed at the University of Pittsburgh on that beautiful autumn Saturday afternoon that my life would change forever! Our children roll their eyes every time I point to the spot where Maria and I met. I remember the minutest details of that meeting. I even remember how good Maria smelled! You, too, have stories about relationships that are important to you.

However, not everyone remembers their first encounter with someone who eventually becomes an important part of their life. What matters is that we consciously deepen our relationship with them. This is especially true in our relationship with God. Having passed through the gate that is Jesus Christ, we move from knowing about God to knowing God. In so doing we realize we are on this journey with him, his "freedom trail" for our lives. Embrace your journey with God.

WITH

Running a Different Race

I had the opportunity to compete in an orienteering challenge in college. As a part of an Army ROTC (Reserve Officers' Training Corps) class we were taught how to use a compass and map to navigate a predetermined course. The race, through the wooded hilltop of a nearby forest, required us to use these guidance tools to navigate to ten markers, over several miles, as fast as possible. Competitors started at staggered intervals, so no one could follow another person through the course. The point was to find your own way.

At my appointed start time, I ran up the hill and quickly found the first marker. I consulted my map and compass and headed off toward the second marker. Halfway through the race I thought I was doing well because I had passed a number of other competitors.

Then I realized I was lost. I had to stop running to figure out where I had veered off course. I wandered around the woods trying to find my bearings. I got turned around once or twice and thought about following someone else but realized they might be lost as well. Using my compass and map, I got back on track. I reached the next marker and eventually crossed the finish line. Unlike a typical race, you don't immediately know who won. Because of the staggered start times, everyone's final race time needed to be calculated.

When the results were announced, I was both disappointed and excited to have finished second. If only I hadn't gotten lost! Somehow, I had done well despite my lack of expertise in orienteering.

When we begin our journey with God we find ourselves in a similar kind of "race." It isn't like a typical race on a track or road. No, our journey with God requires a willingness to embark on an adventure without traditional markings and directions. Additionally, we can't fixate on the finish line because we need to remain in the moment to ensure we stay on course. Ultimately, the challenge is to learn to trust our guide, just as I did with my compass.

A Different Kind of Compass

The handheld magnetic compass I carried through the woods had been invented over 2,000 years ago. The needle of a compass is guided toward the magnetic north of the earth. The compass provides a focal point that guides directional decisions. Think about how we as humans interact with a compass. We are not able to sense or feel the magnetic field that is all around us. Therefore, we need an external instrument to orient us. Essentially, a compass equips us with the ability to connect with a greater force, the earth's magnetic field.

The compass, although ancient in its origins and seemingly old-fashioned in our wired world, can be an effective tool for guidance. But the compass is obsolete because we have GPS, right? The Global Positioning System (GPS) provides us with a different kind of guidance. With the satellite guidance available to us in our car or on our smart phone, we are able to navigate anywhere. We simply type in or say where we want to go, and GPS gives us highly detailed, step-by-step and turn-by-turn instructions from one location to another. As long as we are in receiving range of the system's satellites, all we have to do is follow the directions of our chosen, computer-generated and accented voice to our destination. A compass, on the other hand, keeps us properly oriented but does not provide step-by-step instructions as GPS does; it only points us toward our next step.

Now think about all of this from a spiritual perspective. I remember the beautiful fall foliage and the sound of the crunching leaves as I ran up and down the hills that day. Throughout the race I was exposed to many distractions and alternative routes. To remain on course, I had to trust my compass. Even after getting lost, I used the compass to reestablish my bearings and get back on course. This same lesson holds true as we journey with God. We need guidance to stay on God's path, despite the myriad of alternative routes and distractions.

The good news is that God has provided us with the Holy Spirit. When we are in relationship with God, we have the Holy Spirit available to us as an inner guide. Just as we learn to use a compass, we can learn to "listen" to what the Holy Spirit is telling us. This won't be as easy as following the computerized voice of our GPS. We need to develop the ability to hear and trust in the Holy Spirit as our inner guide.

The amazing thing is that this "inner compass" is not driven by an impersonal magnetic force of the earth, but by the Spirit of God that placed the earth on its axis and set it spinning in the first place. Think about that for a moment! This power within us is the God of all creation, the God who sent his Son to die for our sins, the God who raised his Son from the dead and who sent his Spirit to guide us.

The Spirit with Us

Before he suffered and died, on the night he was arrested, Jesus said to his disciples:

I will ask the Father, and he will give you another Advocate to be with you always, the Spirit of truth, which the world cannot accept, because it neither sees nor knows it. But you know it, because it remains with you, and will be in you.
John 14:16-17

The story of Jesus' intimate last supper with his twelve disciples is one of the few events that are detailed in all four of the Gospels: Matthew, Mark, Luke and John. John's version spans four chapters as Jesus shares significant insights with his closest friends. In the verse above, Jesus speaks of the identity of God as three persons. While he doesn't use the term Trinity, Jesus speaks of all three members. God the Father is the creator, Jesus came as the deliverer and redeemer, and the Holy Spirit was sent as the one who guides us into God's truths on our journey.

Jesus promised that his Spirit would *"be with you always"* and that his Spirit will actually *"be in you."* Every day that we journey with God is a different kind of race, and we are equipped with a guide, infinitely more powerful than a compass, the Holy Spirit. We must continually grow in our relationship with the Holy Spirit in order to know how he guides us. But how can we be certain that we know the Holy Spirit? The Apostle Paul, upon visiting the church in Ephesus, asked the disciples if they had received the Holy Spirit:

"Did you receive the holy Spirit when you became believers?" They answered him, "We have never even heard that there is a holy Spirit."   *Acts 19:2*

Paul helped the new believers to understand that the Holy Spirit exists and then...

*...when Paul laid [his] hands on them, the holy Spirit came
upon them...*   *Acts 19:6*

While the Spirit can be confirmed upon us through the laying on of hands, knowing the Holy Spirit in an ongoing, personal relationship is a completely unique part of our journey with God.

Sidewalk Epiphany

One day as my friend and I walked on the sidewalk in front of my house on the way to his car he asked me, "So how is your relationship with each person of the Trinity?"

Imagine him continuing his walk alone as I stood frozen in my path. "What's wrong?" he turned and asked. "I never thought of it that way," I answered, somewhat thunderstruck. Wow—talk about an epiphany! We can have an intimate relationship with each person: the Father, the Son and the Holy Spirit.

Over the years, I've taught a course about the fundamentals of the Christian faith. I share my Sidewalk Epiphany story during the course because of the question it poses. I love to see the looks on people's faces when I ask the question, "How is your relationship with each person of the Trinity?" Invariably people describe all kinds of ways that they relate to the Father and the Son, but many are challenged to describe their relationship with the Holy Spirit. That is why during the course we lay hands on people and pray, "Be filled with the Holy Spirit." It is humbling to observe God's Spirit ministering to those who are open to knowing him. However, this is not a one-time experience. And it may not feel like an experience at all.

Capture Your Moment

This might be a good time to stop and ask God to fill you with his Holy Spirit. Make it a simple prayer of faith. Trust that God will hear your prayer. Be filled with the Holy Spirit. So how is your relationship with each person of the Trinity?

Jesus promised that his Spirit "*...remains with you, and will be in you.*" Trust that the Father has delivered on his Son's promise to send the Holy Spirit to be with you on your journey. It is in the fulfillment of this promise that our understanding of our identity begins to change.

Our Changing Nature...To Be Like Christ

As we journey with God, we begin the process of becoming more like him. Moses' experience is once again instructive to us. Moses was born an Israelite slave, raised as an Egyptian prince and made his living as a Midianite shepherd. These experiences defined Moses' identity. Moses met God at the burning bush and he embarked on a new journey, with a greater understanding of his true identity as a child of God. God promised that he would be with Moses. God empowered him by enhancing Moses' tool of trade, the shepherd's staff. Moses responded to God's call and he learned to trust God. As Moses stepped forward in faith, God performed miraculous feats to free his people. Moses embraced his true identity as God's child and he humbly submitted to God's plan for his life. In so doing, Moses was continually transformed into the person God created him to be. God does the same with you and me as we journey forward in the power of the Holy Spirit.

The New Testament story of the conversion of Saul provides a vivid example of how a person is changed upon coming to know Jesus.

> *On his journey, as he was nearing Damascus, a light from the sky suddenly flashed around him. He fell to the ground and heard a voice saying to him, "Saul, Saul, why are you persecuting me?" He said, "Who are you, sir?" The reply came, "I am Jesus, whom you are persecuting. Now get up and go into the city and you will be told what you must do."* Acts 9:3-6

After meeting Jesus personally, Saul went from violently persecuting Jesus' church in an attempt to destroy it, to surrendering himself to build the church for God. Saul, also known as Paul, provided his "resume" that defined his impressive identity—and then he explicitly stated how little it all meant after he came to know Jesus.

> *If anyone else thinks he can be confident in flesh, all the more can I. Circumcised on the eighth day, of the race of Israel, of the tribe of Benjamin, a Hebrew of Hebrew parentage, in observance of the law a Pharisee, in zeal I persecuted the church, in righteousness based on the law I was blameless. But whatever gains I had, these I have come to consider a loss because of Christ. More than that, I even consider everything as a loss because*

of the supreme good of knowing Christ Jesus my Lord.
Philippians 3:4-8 (Emphasis added.)

Paul spoke from personal experience as one who was transformed upon meeting Jesus. The definition of the word "transform" is to change completely or essentially in composition or structure. Let's return to the definition of identity, which means sameness of essential character. Our identity is transformed when we are in relationship with Jesus Christ. Our most essential character transforms as we become more like Christ.

After meeting Jesus, Paul grew in his understanding of who he was authentically created to be along with God's plan for his life as a missionary to the world beyond Israel. Jesus' Spirit sent Paul on three missionary journeys to spread the message that Jesus is the Son of God who died, rose from the dead, and ascended back to heaven. Many of the New Testament letters are attributed to Paul as he continued to communicate with the early Christian churches. In these letters, Paul made it clear that the essential character of believers in Christ is transformed. In his second letter to the church in Corinth, Paul says:

So whoever is in Christ is a new creation: the old things have passed away; behold, new things have come.
2 Corinthians 5:17

By using the phrase "new creation," Paul is emphasizing that a profound change has occurred with those who come into relationship with God in Christ. Creation infers beginning. As we explored in the **Our** section of the book, in the beginning, God created humanity in his image. Our essential character— our identity—is like God's. However, Adam and Eve's disobedience resulted in a sinful nature that pursues a false identity. In Christ, we overcome the sinful nature, and we begin anew on our journey to become like Christ.

In a letter to the church in Ephesus, Paul explains this dynamic between the old and the new as a transformative process within each believer:

...you should put away the old self of your former way of life, corrupted through deceitful desires, and be renewed in the spirit of your minds, and put on the new self, created in God's way in righteousness and holiness of truth.
Ephesians 4:22-24

This transformative process to live like Christ is ongoing and it is not without its challenges. As we journey with Christ, it is important to acknowledge that our old self, guided by deceitful desires, needs to be overcome. Even as we mature in our growing relationship with Christ, the temptation to veer off course and to pursue a false identity continues. We need a guide to help us stay on course as we pursue our true identity in Christ in our own unique way. The Holy Spirit is that guide; he is the person Jesus promised to help us navigate this inner, transformative journey.

On my own journey with God I have grown in my understanding of who I am in Christ. In one particularly surprising instance I clearly felt the Spirit's guiding hand.

A Navigational Tool

It was 4:41 a.m. and I lay in bed wide awake. I had just resigned from my job because of a mysterious illness. I was in a panic about not having a job and I cried out to God, "What am I going to do?" The answer came quickly and clearly as the Holy Spirit spoke to my heart: "Write the book."

That was not what I expected to hear! I got out of bed, grabbed a pen and paper and began writing. I knew immediately what the title of the book was and that there were to be four sections, one for each of the words of the title. *Our Journey WITH God* began to take shape in the cold, quiet darkness of that December morning.

I share this story with you for a couple of reasons. First, it marks a profound turning point in my journey with God as he continued to transform me. For ten years, much of my identity was defined by my role as a director of religious education for three churches near my home. My resignation due to health issues signaled a definite new direction as I stepped out in faith toward an unknown destination. Second, I sensed that the Holy Spirit was guiding me on this part of my journey as my writing progressed from page to page. In particular, this section of the book presented an especially surprising message. Initially, each letter of the word "W-I-T-H" jumped out at me. I wrote the letters vertically and four words immediately came to mind, each beginning with one of the letters:

Willing
Intimate
Trusting
Humble

On our journey with God we need to be willing, intimate, trusting and humble. That made sense. I spent some time substituting other words, but these four continued to resonate with me. I thought there must be more than just the basic meanings of these words. Sensing the Spirit's lead, I remembered my college orienteering challenge. That is when I reconfigured the letters into the shape of a compass.

W

H   I

T

One final adjustment and everything fell into place:

I

W   T

H

I made the last change in the placement of the letters when I realized that the "I" representing our intimate relationship with God must be our "true north." Everything needs to point to him. God, by his Holy Spirit, is that life-giving and guiding force who we need to know, on whom we need to rely. Additionally, the shift of the letter "I" to the top of the compass placed the "W" of willing at the western point. We should let our will set like the sun and allow God's guiding Spirit to lead us to his will. The "T" of trust then moved to the eastern orientation. We need to trust God in the newness of each moment, each day, just as we trust that the sun will rise in the east each morning. Finally, the "H" of humble belonged at the southern point. We must remain humbly grounded at the foot of the cross of Jesus. That was the birth of the WITH Compass.

I was excited to see the Holy Spirit in all aspects of the WITH Compass. Just as important, I could see Jesus' journey embedded in the compass as well. Jesus, who humbly became man out of an intimate, loving relationship with his Father in order to willingly suffer and die on the cross, trusted that by the Holy Spirit, God would raise him from the dead.

The WITH Compass provides us with an understanding of, and ability to live intentionally in, this most unique of all relationships. It does so by focusing our attention on the guidance of the Holy Spirit in our lives. The **Our** section of the book emphasized that, created in God's image and likeness, we have the opportunity to live our authentic identity. In the **Journey** section, we looked extensively at the concept of story and what it means to *know* God. We journeyed through the stories of God's people that all intersect at the cross of Jesus. As we continue through the **WITH** section, we will actively and intentionally seek God's Holy Spirit for ongoing guidance on our own unique journey.

Guided by the WITH Compass

I haven't used a compass since my orienteering challenge over 35 years ago, so admittedly, I am not an expert. In fact, I went online to refresh my memory as I was looking for some-

Thank you for
purchasing
Our Journey WITH God.

It is my prayer
that God leads you
on a journey to your
authentic identity
&
unique purpose
in Him.

Blessings,

JOE ✦ KILLIAN
Insights for navigating your journey with God

www.joekillian.com

n the WITH Compass. However, the
s and concepts confused and over-
l I returned to the basic description
ng clicked.
lent used for orientation and naviga-
n I going? That's it!! The simplicity of
e the essence of the function of the
le question of the Holy Spirit, "Where
ing our need to be oriented toward
'Where am I going?" announces our
or, the Holy Spirit. In the language of
d answering these questions would
rings," which refers to the compre-
environment or situation. Just as a
our bearings as we travel, the Holy
rent position, environment or situ-
direction we should go next on our
ng proficient with a compass takes
r relationship with the Holy Spirit
ell.
help us to develop the discipline of
Holy Spirit. This is the mindset we
need to have on our journey with God. It is a new and different way of living. We live, acknowledging that God is the beginning of all that is good, and we seek him for guidance in every aspect of our lives. Where am I? Where am I going? These navigational

questions will be repeated as we explore the concepts of the four WITH Compass points: Willing, Intimate, Trusting and Humble. We will do so with a desire to develop a deeper, more familiar relationship with the Father, Son and especially the Holy Spirit. Prepare to embark on an inner journey of transformation while navigating the uncertainty of the world in which we live. I invite you to "grab your compass" and join me on an exciting journey.

WILLING

Willing is defined as something being done, borne or accepted by choice or without reluctance. Making a willing choice means that we are not forced to do so. Because we make choices from our God-given free will, we want to continually grow in our willingness to live as he desires. Returning to God's four truths discussed in the **Our** section, we know that he created us with the free will to choose for ourselves between good and evil. God's desire is that we willingly obey his commandments and choose him because he is good.

But this obedience is not forced upon us. God ultimately desires that we choose him out of love. While our understanding of God's commandments begins with these truths, Jesus emphasized this love when he was asked which was the greatest of all commandments:

> *You shall love the Lord your God with all your heart, with all your soul, with all your mind, and with all your strength.*
>
> *Mark 12:30*

It is in this love that our response to God's commandments and plans shift from a dutiful obedience to a willing surrender.

If you've made the decision to surrender your life to God as we discussed in **Journey**, you've already made the single most willing choice you can make for God. That step through Jesus, the gate, set you on a new course—a course in which knowing and doing the will of God is an opportunity to become the person God created you to be.

Jesus explained to his disciples the deeper meaning of this loving obedience:

> *If you keep My commandments, you will abide in My love;*
> *just as I have kept My Father's commandments and abide*
> *in His love. These things I have spoken to you so that My*
> *joy may be in you, and that your joy may be made full.*
> *John 15:10-11*

God's love is foundational to our journey as Christians. As willing followers of Christ, we can experience the joy of God's love as we lovingly seek to do his will. The Willing point on the WITH Compass encourages us to willingly seek the Holy Spirit's guidance so that we can remain on God's path.

Willingness vs. Willfulness

What causes us to choose to leave God's path? The answer often lies in the difference between our willingness and will-fulness. Understanding this difference shines a light on the significance of our choices and it highlights our need for a guide.

The parent-child relationship can be instructional to our understanding of the dynamic between willfulness and willingness. Parents experience this dynamic when the word "no" becomes their toddler's favorite answer to every request. Our willfulness, demonstrated in this childish behavior, is apparent in humans at a very early age. Our neighbor described this well when talking about her 18-month-old granddaughter. She said the toddler's favorite words were "no" and "mine." "No" defines rebellion against authority, and "mine" demonstrates selfishness.

Think of the willful toddler, arms crossed, face set with determination to resist her mother's request. Sarah exhibited a strong will from an early age. Three of her frequently used words as a toddler, "I do it," demonstrated her desire to be self-sufficient. Of course, self-sufficiency can be a great asset but when taken to the extreme it can become problematic, especially in our relationship with God. Willfulness is a posture of seeking to attain something we desire or avoiding something we don't want to do. This emanates from our self-will. The issue is when this self-will is exerting itself in one of two unhealthy ways. First, as we explored in the **Our** section of the book, we sin out of our selfish desires. We willfully choose to disobey God. Second, our willful desire to be self-sufficient can cause us to resist help, support and guidance when we need it. As adults, this can manifest in our willful pride, our stubbornness and even dogged determination to get something done. These behaviors can be detrimental to our relationship with God. God desires that we rely on him and surrender to him.

Now think of another toddler, arms outstretched, face aglow with glee at the return of his mother. Maria and I smile warmly at the thought of 18-month-old Joey reaching his arms out and saying, "Hold you me." His desire was to be with us, and he was willingly giving himself over to us. Willingness is a receptive posture of openness oriented toward something out of self-surrender. As we mature in life and particularly on our journey with God, we need to grow beyond our self-centered, strong-willed ways. Being willing means we receptively "open our arms" to God who loves us, with a desire to do his will.

From Willfulness to Willingness

One of the most challenging aspects of parenting is learning how to discipline children in ways that teach them to submit to appropriate authority. Have you ever observed the behavior of a spoiled child who gets their way by throwing a tantrum in the checkout line at the grocery store? I've found myself rooting for the parent to remain strong despite the disruptive behavior of the screaming child. If a child does not learn to surrender their will to the higher authority of the wiser parent, they can become completely self-absorbed.

Biblically, we are encouraged to begin this process when children are young:

Train the young in the way they should go; even when old,
they will not swerve from it. Proverbs 22:6

At the same time, effective, Godly discipline that trains the will needs to be balanced with love that nurtures the child. This balance is achieved through loving, positive affirmation of the child's authentic identity combined with corrective discipline. This approach provided Maria and me a way of raising our children lovingly, despite the fact that disciplining them was difficult.

I once disciplined young Sarah for having broken a family rule about telling the truth. I reminded her that her willful choice to lie was the reason punishment was necessary. After I punished her, I hugged her and told her I loved her. I was doing my best to clearly give Sarah the message that she needed to submit her will to the authority of our family "commandments." Because I had followed through on the punishment, she learned that there were consequences to her choices. This taught her to think twice about not telling the truth in the future.

This was a painful experience for both Sarah and me. Even though I explained that I was following through on my punishment because I loved her, Sarah was too young to fully comprehend the deeper meaning of my actions. My actions were intended to train Sarah's will while nurturing her spirit, which in turn developed her desire to submit out of love. As Sarah matured, she came to appreciate my actions and to love me for them.

Coming to know the dynamic process of moving from willfulness to willingness is critical to our journey with God. When we realize that God's intention is to draw us closer to him through this process, we can learn to submit to him willingly, out of love.

Loving Discipline

Because of humanity's sinful nature, there will be times when we need to be corrected. God, our Father, lovingly disciplines us, his children. The letter to the Hebrews provides us with this understanding:

> *My son, do not disdain the discipline of the Lord or lose heart when reproved by him; for whom the Lord loves, he disciplines;*   *Hebrews 12:5-6*

God disciplines us because he loves us and wants us to remain in his love as we journey with him. In his infinitely patient love, God gives us the opportunity to submit to his will and keep his commandments. However, temptation often rears its ugly head, and we are caught in that same doubtful dialogue that Adam and Eve experienced in the garden. This is when rationalization becomes our worst enemy. It's like seeing that the compass is pointing us in one direction and deciding to walk in another. Duh!! And yet we do it, often! The obvious consequence is that we get lost. When we disobey his commandments, God allows the consequences of our willful choices to discipline us. As you and I wrestle with our will, we need to ask the Holy Spirit to show us where we are being willfully sinful. One purpose of the WITH Compass is to remind us to do so.

Just as parents seek to train the will of their children, God desires that we lovingly submit to his will for our lives. He does not force us into submission. Even as he disciplines us, God nurtures our spirit so that we can become more like Christ and grow to be the authentic person he created us to be.

Redirecting Our Path

In the process of becoming more like Christ, we are led to God's unique path for our lives. With our eyes focused on the Willing point of the WITH Compass, we can ask the Holy Spirit for direction and strength to make the right choices.

I experienced God lovingly redirecting me while I was working as an independent business consultant and trainer. I had worked hard to establish my business and at times had been so busy I could barely keep up with the demands of my clients. The business had been growing over the years, but I was struggling personally.

Looking out of my office window on a cold, rainy October day as the last of the leaves were being washed from the trees, I realized that it was time to let go of my business. I knew deep down God was calling me to something new, but it wasn't until I said the words, "This is your business now, God," that I had truly submitted my will to his. Those words, which I tearfully spoke as a willing submission of my whole self to God, allowed me to move forward on my journey with him. It was simultaneously a will-breaking and spirit-filling moment. Not only was I learning that God had a plan for me, I was also beginning to embrace who I was authentically created to be in Christ Jesus.

In Paul's letter to the Ephesians he captured this dynamic beautifully:

*For we are God's masterpiece. He has created us anew
in Christ Jesus, so we can do the good things He planned
for us long ago.*   *Ephesians 2:10*

As we leave our old self behind and as God leads and guides us on his path, we participate in an exciting adventure. The stories of the Bible and throughout church history provide us with countless examples of those who willingly submitted to God. This process never ends for each of us.

While I often struggle to listen to the promptings of the Holy Spirit, I continue to seek his guidance in submitting my will to God. In so doing, I pursue his plans for my life. I believe that for me, the book you are holding in your hands is one of God's "redirected plans" coming to fruition.

Sarah's example and mine demonstrate two primary ways in which our wills are formed. Sarah's experience was more corrective in nature, because she had willfully chosen to disobey. The shaping of Sarah's will was intended to teach her to willingly choose the right path. My experience shows how God redirected my plans, giving me the opportunity to choose to submit to his will for my future. Although this was not a case of me living sinfully outside the will of God, it illustrates how God redirected my path. A Father's love was at the root of both. God's actions are intended to mold and guide us. Regardless of whether they are corrective or directive, God desires that we choose to journey with him willingly—out of love. To help us, he has given us his Holy Spirit as a guide for the journey.

The WITH Compass can function as a handy reminder to seek the Holy Spirit in all kinds of situations. At the same time, it is not necessary to bring every decision to the Holy Spirit. Choosing what we are going to eat for breakfast does not require great discerning prayer time to know whether God wants us to eat cereal, yogurt or pancakes. As we journey with God, we want to be aware of the Holy Spirit's guiding voice, especially in significant matters of the heart. This is a lifelong process that we can grow in as we learn to rely on the Holy Spirit for guidance.

Using the WITH Compass–Willing

With an understanding of what it means to be willing, you are now poised to move ahead on your journey—willingly. The purpose of the WITH Compass is to encourage you to assess your willingness to submit to God's will in your current circumstances as well as for your future.

With your will in mind, ask the Holy Spirit the following questions as they pertain to you becoming more Christ-like:

- Where am I?
- Where am I going?

Wait on the Spirit to speak. This may be challenging because silence can be uncomfortable. Listen to your heart. If you seek the voice of the Holy Spirit, you are apt to occasionally hear that your will needs to be submitted to God's. You may hear the Spirit convict you of your willfulness that has lead you into sin. As difficult as this might be, rest assured that God wants you to repent and return to his path. In a different way you may hear from the Spirit that it is time to move in a new direction. This may come as a surprise and you will need to willingly step out in faith as God prompts you. The key is to listen with an open and receptive "posture" that allows God to transform and guide you.

The WITH Compass can help you to acknowledge God before you make your choices. By becoming familiar and comfortable with this tool, you can stay oriented toward God, as you willingly allow him to be the navigator on your journey with him.

Capture Your Moment

Did it ever occur to you that God surrenders *his* will for our lives—to you and me? Reflect on that for a while and capture your moment.

Willing Prayer

Allow the Holy Spirit and the Willing compass point to direct you toward, and keep you on, God's path. You can do so by submitting your will to God in prayer. The words of the Lord's Prayer, which Jesus gave us, focus our will on the will of God the Father:

"This is how you are to pray: Our Father in heaven, hallowed be your name, your kingdom come, your will be done, on earth as in heaven. Give us today our daily bread; and forgive us our debts, as we forgive our debtors; and do not subject us to the final test, but deliver us from the evil one."

Matthew 6:9-13

INTIMATE

Intimate can be defined in numerous ways:

- belonging to or characterizing one's deepest nature
- marked by very close association, contact, or familiarity
- marked by a warm friendship developing through long association, suggesting informal warmth or privacy
- of a very personal or private nature

Having been created in the image and likeness of God, our deepest nature—our identity—belongs to him. When we come to know God, we can grow closer to him. Even though Jesus was their teacher and leader, he called his disciples friends. He wants to have a friendship with you and me as well. That friendship with God can be as deeply personal and private as any. Can we experience this kind of intimacy with God? Absolutely!

Intimacy begins with intentional, dedicated time with God. He is ever present, so we can seek intimacy anywhere and at any time. The key is to consciously choose to pursue intimacy with God.

Draw near to God, and He will draw near to you.

James 4:8

Drawing near to God is not a physical act, although we may need to physically move to a quiet place to eliminate distractions. Drawing near to God is most significantly an act of the heart. Our desire for this closeness is rooted in God's love for us.

God is love, and whoever remains in love remains in God and God in him.   *1 John 4:16*

Out of love, God initiates everything in our relationship. His Spirit guides us to pursue intimacy with him. The Intimate point on the WITH Compass is meant to orient our heart toward God's Holy Spirit in all circumstances and to encourage us to seek an even deeper relationship with him.

True Intimacy

Ever since I first met Maria, I've wanted to be in her presence. Even brief times apart leave me pining to be with her again. Maria and I have a little phrase to express to one another that we are experiencing a sense of intimacy. "I feel close to you." When one of us utters these simple words, the resulting smile is always warm and genuine. For me this is one of the most powerful and intimate things I experience in my marriage and my life. When Maria shares her heart with me, we experience a deep connection that is rooted in our love for one another. All aspects of the definition of intimacy are exhibited in our relationship. Having been married for over 30 years, we **lovingly belong** to one another. A **closeness and familiarity** exists between us that is truly unique to our relationship. People often comment on the **warm friendship** we share with one another. We connect at a deeply **personal and private** level. Maria and I are blessed to experience true intimacy. And while our relationship is intimate, we acknowledge that it isn't always positive and happy. We struggle at times, but that doesn't mean we don't love one another. Most importantly, our love, grounded in true intimacy, is much deeper than feelings. The good news is that true intimacy can be experienced with God, because he initiates the relationship.

We love because he first loved us. 1 *John 4:19*

We need to respond to God's always available and present love. We do so by intentionally and passionately pursuing an intimate connection with God.

Girlfriends and Telephone Cords

Back when I was a teenager, telephones still had rotary dials and were firmly affixed to the wall. That meant that if I wanted to talk with my girlfriend I had no choice but to do so on the one phone in our house that hung on the wall in our small kitchen. I remember when we first got an extra-long phone cord. I know I drove my mom crazy as I stretched the cord to its limits in a vain attempt to find some privacy. The level of intimate communication with my girlfriend was constrained by the length of that coiled cord. Not only that, but once I hung up the phone our connection was lost.

Many people pray this way. We set the time aside and communicate during our prayer time but as soon as we get up from our "prayer spot" we lose our connection with God. True intimacy doesn't have to end when we complete our prayer time. Prayer can and should be an ongoing process. Today we live in a wireless world that is dependent on technology to keep us connected. Unlike the cellular phone companies, the Holy Spirit provides the absolute best coverage possible—and he never drops a call. In other words, we need to go wireless with the Holy Spirit!

Remain in Him

This is how we know that we remain in him and he in us,
that he has given us of his Spirit.   *1 John 4:13*

Try this simple early prayer of the church: "Come Holy Spirit." Your attention is drawn to God. When we are focused on him, we are directed away from the ways of the world. Because he has given us his Holy Spirit we can remain in intimate contact with God throughout our day.

Jesus modeled this for us as he sought to remain intimate with his Father. He continually spent time with him even if it meant he did so in the middle of the night. On numerous occasions in the Gospels we hear of Jesus going to be alone with his Father.

Rising very early before dawn, he left and went off to a
deserted place, where he prayed.   *Mark 1:35*

In those days he departed to the mountain to pray, and
he spent the night in prayer to God.   *Luke 6:1*

We can't be intimate if we don't spend time together! While Jesus did go away to be with his Father, there were also occasions where he demonstrated a closeness to him even in the midst of a crowd. In those times that we don't feel God's presence, we need to rest in the fact that he is still there. He remains, so it is up to us to seek to be with him, intimately.

Barriers to Intimacy with God

But Jesus cried out again in a loud voice, and gave up his
spirit. And behold, the veil of the sanctuary was torn in
two from top to bottom.   *Matthew 27:50-51*

When Jesus died on the cross, the sins of all humanity were forgiven by his willing sacrifice. In that same moment, the veil of the temple was torn. God had instructed the Israelites to design the temple with a large, thick veil that separated the Holy of Holies from the rest of the temple. It was in the Holy of Holies, behind the veil, that the presence of God dwelled. The veil was the barrier between God and sinful humanity, who could not physically be in his presence. Jesus' sacrificial death removed the barrier separating humanity from God's presence. Once God sent his Holy Spirit, our access to him was available all the time.

Yet, sin is still the primary spiritual barrier between us and an intimate relationship with God. In our flesh we continue to choose to disobediently sin, which creates a spiritual separation from God. Remember the story of the little boy who turned his back on a pleasantly surprised teacher to explain what happens when we sin? When we sin, choosing self over God, it is as if we are turning our back on him. If we think of it literally, selfishly turning our back on another person would break the intimate connection we had with them. In order to remain intimate with God we must turn back to him in the midst of our sinfulness. The Holy Spirit, acting like a compass, convicts us that we have left God's path and he prompts us to turn back to our merciful Father. He is always there, but we need to acknowledge that we need his forgiveness and repent of our sinful ways.

Living in an intimate relationship with God is a choice. That is why living in today's world is such a challenge. The temptations and distractions are endless. From the moment we wake up in the morning until we go to bed at night we are making choices. The more we live in intimate communion with God the more inclined we are to choose him instead of self and the world. When we focus on the WITH Compass, the Holy Spirit can prompt us to seek intimacy with God.

Intimate Ways

A foundation of dedicated time is the starting point to an intimate relationship with God. Morning quiet time with God is my preferred way. Being a morning person helps, because I often wake up before the sun comes up when no one else is awake. Those early morning times of intimacy with God have become treasured moments on my journey with him. What if you're not a morning person? I encourage you to start small with some intentional God time. Allow this to orient you for the day. Pray as you commute. Offer God quick prayers of gratitude throughout your day.

Evenings can work well because God is always ready and waiting for you, and you can ask the Holy Spirit to assess your day. If you're able, get on your knees beside your bed at night and seek him. The intentional, heartfelt desire to be intimate with God is what matters most.

Few things in our journey with God will draw us closer to him than his word. The Bible is infinitely more than a book.

Indeed, the word of God is living and effective, sharper than any two-edged sword, penetrating even between soul and spirit, joints and marrow, and able to discern reflections and thoughts of the heart. Hebrews 4:12

This verse "coincidentally" kept popping up for me in the very early days of my journey with God. Its message encapsulates the incredible nature of God's word. Whether we need tender love in times of trial and suffering or chastisement in times of sin, God's word speaks to the depths of our hearts. Knowing God's word allows us to know him more intimately. This is why the proclamation of God's word has been an integral part of the church for 2,000 years. Our participation in a church where we continually hear God's word is a necessary part of our journey as Christians. But because God's word is living and effective, we also need to

100

make our own personal journey into the Bible, trusting the Holy Spirit to guide us.

Since God created us, he knows best how to approach us. He does so by his Spirit. Each of us in our authentic self has to find our way to intimacy with God. God can connect with us while we read a Christian book, as you're doing right now. Or he may speak to our heart while we listen to Christian music. By his Spirit, God is as readily able to speak to us in the middle of a traffic jam as he is in a business meeting or in a grocery store checkout line. And few things speak of God more powerfully than his natural creation that is all around us. We simply must stop and acknowledge God in it. Because God is everywhere, the ways in which we can be intimate with him are countless.

Using the WITH Compass–Intimate

What an incredible blessing it is to know God and to be intimate with him. You have an opportunity to grow in intimacy with him. The purpose of the WITH Compass is to encourage you to continually seek intimacy with God regardless of where you are and what you are doing.

With intimacy in mind, ask the Holy Spirit the following questions as they pertain to you becoming more Christ-like:

- Where am I?
- Where am I going?

This is where you allow the Holy Spirit to speak to you regarding your level of intimacy with God. We can be overwhelmed at times by the powerful presence of God. Or we may hear the Spirit convict us of some sinful behavior that has become a barrier to intimacy with God. An open and receptive posture is again important because it demonstrates our desire to be close to God.

The WITH Compass can help us to acknowledge God as we seek to enter into his presence. By becoming familiar and comfortable with this tool we can remain intimate with God, allowing him to guide us as we navigate on our journey.

Capture Your Moment

Everything on our journey with God starts with knowing God. Knowing God intimately is the basis of our growing relationship with him. What does that mean to you today?

Intimate Prayer

Prayer is the foundation to our intimate relationship with God. Ask the Spirit to lead you:

"Come Holy Spirit. Draw me closer to you, my God."

TRUSTING

Trusting is defined as assured reliance on the character, ability, strength or truth of someone or something. Our trust in God is rooted in our belief that he is who he says he is. The many stories of his people throughout the ages demonstrate God's trustworthiness. In particular, in the Exodus story, God demonstrated his character, ability and strength time and time again. True to his word to Moses, God miraculously delivered on his promise to free the Israelites from bondage in Egypt. Like Moses, God desires that we have complete trust in him.

Trust in the Lord with all your heart and lean not on your own understanding; in all your ways submit to him, and he will make your paths straight. Proverbs 3:5-6
(New International Version)

The trust that God desires of us is actually all-encompassing. The more we trust in God's faithfulness the more trust he will desire and expect from us. As we journey with him we need to grow in our ability to trust him in all things. Our journey with God is a relationship that can be defined by everything from profound realization that he has seen us through something life-threatening to tiny moments of recognition that he is trustworthy in the smallest ways.

We know that all things work for good for those who love God, who are called according to his purpose.
Romans 8:28

Regardless of what happens along the way, we must trust that God is working for our good in the circumstances of our lives. Having a long-term perspective is what allows us to trust God. In his letter to the Romans, Paul made it clear that God's love for us is the defining characteristic of our trust in him:

> For I am convinced that neither death, nor life, nor angels, nor principalities, nor present things, nor future things, nor powers, nor height, nor depth, nor any other creature will be able to separate us from the love of God in Christ Jesus our Lord.   Romans 8:38-39

Paul encourages us that we can have an "assured reliance" in our God. We simply have to seek him out in all situations that we face, trusting in his **character**, **ability** and **strength**. The Trusting point on the WITH Compass orients us to seek the Holy Spirit's guidance to give us the strength to trust God in all circumstances we encounter along the way.

We're Going Skydiving

A few years ago Sarah excitedly gave me my birthday present. I still have the handmade certificate that said, "Get ready, 'cause… we're going skydiving!!!" A month later Sarah and I were on our way up to 13,000 feet with our tandem jumpers. I was the first one out of the airplane's door and it was…indescribable! If you've never taken that leap from 13,000 feet, it's difficult to understand the exhilarating sensation of flying. I know it's actually falling, but it's all in your perspective. It was like nothing I had ever experienced before!

Think of how much trust Sarah and I placed in "others" when we jumped out of that plane. We trusted our lives to everyone from the manufacturers of the plane and the parachute, to the pilot of the plane, and to our tandem jumpers.

Let's go even deeper. We trusted the various laws of physics and aerodynamics. We trusted gravity. In doing so we had an incredible experience. Could things have gone wrong? Absolutely! But we were willing to take the leap, and the results were amazing. Sarah and I both chose to trust all of these things. Maria, Joshua and my Dad all chose to trust gravity over all else. They kept their feet firmly planted on solid ground. Not everyone is a risk-taking thrill-seeker.

When it comes to trusting in God we all must learn to step onto the path he sets before us. That means we will need to step out in faith, trusting in him to see us through whatever comes our way. Skydiving is a pretty extreme example of how we trust. While trusting in God can be pretty extreme at times, it can also be somewhat simplistic. There are countless opportunities for us to trust in God's providence each and every day.

Hand-holding

While visiting with our neighbors I entertained their two little boys, 4 and 3 years old, while Maria chatted with their mom. The boys asked their mom if they could go to see Tanner, our dog. As we walked down their driveway towards our house the boys reflexively reached for my hands. We were about to cross the street and they knew they needed my guidance. Once we stepped into our front yard they both let go of my hands and ran towards the front door. Stopping short of our front porch they sought my assurance before moving closer to Tanner. After a minute of petting our furry dog, the boys were ready to return home. They ran out to the end of our yard and stopped and waited for me to hold their hands and escort them back across the street.

God does the same with us. As we first enter into a relationship with him, it is to be expected that we might experience a little "hand-holding" from God. As we mature, God will call us to greater levels of trust. Peter demonstrated great trust when, at Jesus' command, he stepped out of the boat in the midst of a storm.

> *"Come," he said. Then Peter got out of the boat and began*
> *to walk on the water toward Jesus.*   Matthew 14:29

Even though Jesus was asking him to do the seemingly impossible, Peter trusted that Jesus was in control.

> *But when he saw how [strong] the wind was he became*
> *frightened; and, beginning to sink, he cried out, "Lord,*
> *save me!" Immediately **Jesus stretched out his hand***
> ***and caught him**, and said to him, "O you of little faith,*
> *why did you doubt?"*   Matthew 14:30-31
>   *(Emphasis added.)*

When Peter became fearful of the storm that surrounded him, he called out to Jesus who *"stretched out his hand."* Just as my young neighbors reached out for my hand, we need to do the same with God.

On our journey, God will allow situations to arise that require us to trust him. We may find ourselves on a path that challenges our common sense. We can go the seemingly "safe" route, or we can choose to step out into the unknown with God. We need to rely on God's Holy Spirit to give us the courage to take that trusting leap or to endure a difficult time. Keeping the WITH Compass in mind will help you focus on God and his trustworthiness. We must trust that God is always there for us, regardless of the circumstances and the outcome.

Trusting in Tough Times

Phone calls at 1:45 in the morning are rarely good. Our niece, Hennessey, was calling us from the emergency room. She had just brought our daughter, Sarah, in to the Florida hospital near their apartment because Sarah's heart rate was dangerously elevated. We talked with Hennessey while Sarah was being checked in. Over the next couple of hours, Maria and I sat in our living room praying and crying as we waited for more information. When Hennessey told us that Sarah was being sedated and taken to the intensive care unit in an effort to bring her heart rate back down, we booked a flight.

At 8:30 that morning our plane lifted off from Pittsburgh for the 2 hour and 15-minute flight to Orlando. Up until that point we were able to communicate with Hennessey and her dad, John, Maria's brother. Once we took off there was no phone connection, and the torturous wait had begun.

We continued to pray and after one intense prayer, God gave me peace. This peace washed over me like a wave. I was able to catch my breath for the first time since the phone had rung seven hours earlier. Of course, my prayer was that Sarah would be okay, but God's peace wasn't specifically about that. I tensed and said to him, "Okay, Lord, I trust you. Your will be done. Whatever that might be." He had not given me a guarantee that Sarah was going to be okay, only that I could trust that he would be with us through it all, regardless of what happened. I squeezed Maria's hand as I thanked God.

It was the longest plane flight of our lives—one in which we tried to stay focused on God. Every time emotion threatened to overwhelm me, I turned to him and his Holy Spirit. My mind raced through scenarios, good and bad. When I prayed, God's peace allowed me to focus on him. It can be easy to say we trust in God, especially in good times. But life is not always "good." How are we to respond when bad things happen? In Paul's letter to the Philippians, we find our answer.

Rejoice in the Lord always. I shall say it again: rejoice!
Your kindness should be known to all. The Lord is near.
Have no anxiety at all, but in everything, by prayer and
petition, with thanksgiving, make your requests known

to God. Then the peace of God that surpasses all under-standing will guard your hearts and minds in Christ Jesus.
Philippians 4:4-7

God is sovereign over all things and we need to trust in him in all circumstances. Later that same day the doctor who had admitted Sarah to the ICU gave us the answer to our prayers: "She is going to be okay." Sarah was still sedated, but the doctor was confident that she was past the worst part. Tears of joy filled our eyes as we thanked God.

Countless people have prayed every bit as fervently as we did that day but didn't receive the good news we did. Perhaps you are one of them. We cannot expect to understand why things happen as they do. What we can do is trust that God is sovereign. It is in the most difficult and challenging of times that we must trust that the same God who created the universe can make *"all things work for good."* And that may mean we have to wait—a long time!

Learning to Wait on God

Abraham waited for a son until he was almost 100. Joseph languished in a prison cell for years. Moses lived to be 80 before understanding his true purpose at the burning bush. The length of the wait is not what matters. We can trust God because we have the Holy Spirit with us to comfort and guide us through it all. That includes the joys and victories as well as the heartbreak and uncertainties of life.

Trusting in God means we always look with hope to his purposes for our lives. That does not mean we will not struggle and suffer. It may even mean that death comes to us or a loved one. A friend of mine owns a funeral home. He once shared with me that there is a profound difference between a Christian funeral and one of a non-believer. While grief and pain permeate both, the sense of hope in a Christian funeral is profoundly greater. The reason seems obvious. The families of those who have died, knowing God and his plans for us, trust in his promise of life everlasting in his presence. We as Christians must have a long-term view of life and life after death. This is a critically important element in our ability to trust God. By seeking the Holy Spirit's guidance, Christians are able to see beyond our current circumstances to the hope of a future with God.

For through the Spirit, by faith, we await the hope of righteousness.   *Galatians 5:5*

Instead of asking why our prayers are not being answered, we would be better served by making a different request. We can ask the Holy Spirit to give us the strength and ability to accept the circumstances we find ourselves in, trusting that God is in control. This is what it means to truly trust God.

Finding the Courage to Trust in God

Most likely we will not know where God is leading us on our journey with him. That is why trusting in God takes courage. Ask yourself the question, "Am I willing to be uncomfortable on this journey with God?" This exposes the fears that are keeping us from submitting our will and trusting God. We can become paralyzed by our fears and lose sight that our faith must be in God. This is not to say that we will never doubt or experience fear. Both are normal human reactions. Our challenge is to confront our doubts and fears with assured reliance on God.

David, writer of the Psalms, slayer of the giant Goliath and one of the most courageous of God's warriors, trusted God in the most challenging of circumstances.

When I am afraid, in you I place my trust.   *Psalm 56:4*

David was a wanted fugitive in fear for his life when he wrote this Psalm. His complete trust in God saw him through many battles and attacks, and he was eventually anointed king over all of Israel.

In the moments before Peter stepped out of the boat to walk on water in the midst of the storm, Jesus spoke to the disciples:

Take courage, it is I; do not be afraid.   Matthew 14:27

This is what trusting God is all about: *"...it is I."* These words remind us that Jesus is always with us as he promised. We must learn to consciously seek his Spirit and then take a leap of faith each and every time God calls us to do so. That means we have to trust that when we figuratively step out of the boat or jump out of the plane, he will be there for us. The Holy Spirit, as our guide, will give us the courage we need to trust God in increasingly greater ways than we ever have before.

Using the WITH Compass–Trusting

The great thing about trusting in God is that our trust is rooted in a God who is fully trustworthy. As always, trust begins with God. In trusting God, the purpose of the WITH Compass is to encourage you to seek the Holy Spirit to acknowledge your doubts and fears and to help you step out in faith with and for God.

With trusting in mind, ask the Holy Spirit these questions as they pertain to you becoming more Christ-like:

- Where am I at this moment?
- Where do I go from here?

Listen for the Holy Spirit to remind you of God's trustworthiness. Once we acknowledge our fears and God's trustworthiness, he gives us the courage to trust him regardless of our

110

circumstances. Rest assured that God's plan for you is not only in your best interest but that it is for his glory too. Don't forget to listen with an open and receptive posture that allows God to transform you.

The WITH Compass can bring us the courage and strength we need for our journey, because we are relying on God's Holy Spirit. Trusting on our WITH Compass guides us to wholly place our lives in God's hands. By becoming familiar and comfortable with this tool, we can stay oriented toward God, trusting him to guide us as we navigate on our journey.

Capture Your Moment

Journeying without knowing our destination requires that we trust in our guide. The Holy Spirit is always present, and his role is to be your guide. In what areas of your life are you lacking trust? What holds you back from trusting the Holy Spirit as your guide?

Trusting Prayer

The verse from Proverbs at the beginning of this section provides us with an ideal, journey-oriented prayer. Reworded slightly it reads:

"I trust in you Lord with all my heart and I choose to not lean on my own understanding. I submit to you in all my ways and ask that you make my path straight."

HUMBLE

Humble as an adjective is defined as not proud or haughty, not arrogant or assertive. Additional definitions include: reflecting, expressing or offered in a spirit of deference or submission. Another definition is ranking low in a hierarchy or scale. Taking these in order gives us some interesting insight. To be humble we must begin from a position of having no self-centered pride or arrogance.

He must increase, but I must decrease.   John 3:30

John the Baptist spoke these words as he humbly pointed his followers to Jesus. John had become quite the "rock star" in his time. His following had grown to the point where the authorities were well aware of who he was. And this was in spite of the challenging message he delivered to the people. And yet, John the Baptist was not proud or arrogant and he clearly knew where

112

he ranked. But where does that humility come from? It comes from a spirit oriented toward God above all else.

You have been told, O mortal, what is good, and what the LORD requires of you: Only to do justice and to love goodness, and to walk humbly with your God
Micah 6:8

In defining the greatest commandment, Jesus clearly pointed to our need for deference to God and others. By combining love with a spirit of deference, Jesus helps us to accept a "lower ranking" on the hierarchy scale.

You shall love the Lord your God with all your heart, with all your soul, with all your mind, and with all your strength. The second is this: You shall love your neighbor as yourself. There is no other commandment greater than these.
Mark 12:29-31

The ancient Israelites lived their lives by an extensive list of more than 600 commandments. By emphasizing the loving spirit of God's commandments, Jesus not only challenged the legalistic nature of his culture at that time, he totally shifted its focus. Jesus made it clear that all things were to be done in love from a position of deference to God and others, or in other words, from a humble spirit.

The Humble point on the WITH Compass orients us to humbly seek the Holy Spirit's guidance to love and serve God and others.

I'm Third

A trusted family friend told us that sending her sons to Summer's Best Two Weeks, a Christian sports camp, was one of the best things she, as a parent, had done for her sons. Joey first attended when he was nine years old, and for the next 15 years, the Killian family had at least one child at SB2W. We would drop our campers off on a Sunday, and for the next two weeks, we could only communicate with them through the mail. We placed our complete trust in the counselors and staff at the camp, who we knew placed their trust in God.

Being a sports camp, the competitions pitted the red-clad Romans versus the blue Galatians in a wide variety of team and individual sports. When we picked up the kids two weeks later, we were always overwhelmed by the joyful and yet humble spirit that everyone demonstrated. It was awesome to watch the winning team as they cheered for the losing team. At the end of the cheer both teams would shout in unison, "Who gets the glory? Jesus!" The camp's "I'm Third" motto, rooted in Jesus' greatest commandment, embodies true Christian humility. At SB2W, "God First, Others Second and I'm Third" is more than just a slogan found on a tee shirt. It is at the core of everything that happens there. It is no wonder that the kids have such a transformative experience. "I'm Third" is a phrase that defines the essence of what it means to be humble.

At camp the kids saw this humility demonstrated over and over again. My favorite stories on the car rides home from camp revolved around the humble spirit of the older, more accomplished campers helping others. Seeing this kind of consistent behavior laid the groundwork for an understanding of what it means to be humble. The message to the campers and to all who journey with Christ is that we are to live humbly in service to God and others.

What does humble look like? True humility is one of those things that we recognize when we see it. To be humble is to live from a condition of the heart turned toward God.

> *...humbly regard others as more important than your-*
> *selves...* *Philippians 2:3*

Paul's words seem to be relatively straightforward, but it can be difficult to know what is truly in our hearts.

Humbled

I left the downtown parking garage, unusually early for my client meeting. As I walked through the midday crowd, I felt a prompting to stop and offer to buy a homeless person lunch. I had previously passed by this man in the same spot many times. This prompting was very clear and specific. It wasn't about handing the man some spare change or a couple of dollar bills which I had done before. No, I had even envisioned the deli up the street where I would take him. My thought, before the man came into view was, "Yes. I have the time. If he is there, I'll stop and invite him to the deli."

This happened to me early on my journey with God. A couple of years earlier I had felt called to attend a local Bible School. For three years I took classes full-time while continuing to serve a few of my business clients. In my last semester I was invited to travel to New York City on a mission trip to serve the homeless. I was hesitant to commit to the trip because I was already stretched to my limit juggling family, school and my business clients.

Back to the homeless man on the street. Upon turning the corner, I could see him sitting on the sidewalk up ahead. "Okay, so he is there," I thought. I glanced at my watch, and as I came close to him, I—walked right past. Yep. Never even slowed down. Surprised? I was! I kept right on walking to my client's office. After my meeting I started to feel guilty. Why had I ignored such a clear prompting that I sensed had come from God? "Lord, if the man is still there I promise I'll stop this time." I prayed as I headed back to the parking garage. The man was no longer there. Later that evening I sat down on the couch to read and pray. The words to an old church hymn resonated within me and I opened my Bible to find its message.

> Then the righteous will answer him and say, "Lord, when did we see you hungry and feed you, or thirsty and give you drink? When did we see you a stranger and welcome you, or naked and clothe you? When did we see you ill or in prison, and visit you?" And the king will say to them in reply, "Amen, I say to you, whatever you did for one of these least brothers of mine, you did for me."
>
> Matthew 25:37-40

My opportunity was gone. I felt horrible, selfish, unworthy. I wept. I was too self-absorbed to stop and speak to a homeless person. The self-condemnation came quickly. So much for being committed to live my life for Christ, I lamented. What a model Bible School student I was. I realized that I had been looking for an excuse to say, "No, I don't have the time to go to New York." God had shown me the true condition of my heart. I had been stripped bare before God. Humbled. I kept reading.

> He will answer them, "Amen, I say to you, what you did not do for one of these least ones, you did not do for me." And these will go off to eternal punishment, but the righteous to eternal life.
>
> Matthew 25:45-46

I decided in that moment that I needed to go to New York. I am grateful for the opportunity to do so because that trip changed my life. God's redeeming love gave me a second chance, and I took full advantage of it in New York. In one instance I had the chance to follow the Spirit's prompting. He led me to a heroin-addicted, homeless man on a street corner in Harlem. And the Holy Spirit helped me to share my story. Not the one of walking past the homeless man back home, but the story of why I was truly in New York, my commitment to live my life for Christ. After spending time with this addicted man, he somewhat abruptly got up and said, "I need to get back to the shelter before they stop serving lunch." I asked if I could walk with him for a little and he said yes. As we crossed the street, the man stopped and looked me in the eye and said, "Why do you people do this?" My answer came quickly. "Because I love you. Because Jesus loves you." He paused, shook his head incredulously, and walked on. Thank you, Jesus, for loving us all.

A tool like the WITH Compass might have prompted me to stop and interact with that first homeless man. Even though I didn't stop, God used my unwillingness to show me my lack of humility—the true condition of my heart. My hope is that the WITH Compass will prompt you to ask the Holy Spirit to help you choose to humbly serve those that God places in your path.

The Foot of the Cross

The Holy Spirit had convicted me for walking past the homeless man he had placed in my path. That night I sought forgiveness at the foot of Jesus' cross for my disobedient and selfish sin. Because Jesus died to self on that cross, we must do the same. Paul described this dynamic to the Galatian church:

I have been crucified with Christ; yet I live, no longer I, but Christ lives in me; insofar as I now live in the flesh, I live by faith in the Son of God who has loved me and given himself up for me.   *Galatians 2:19-20*

It is at the foot of the cross, where we offer ourselves to Christ, that we find the humility we need to sacrificially die to self. That is where we also learn to live and love as Jesus did. In a profoundly humble act, Jesus took on the role of the lowliest household servant and washed his disciples' feet! He did so on the night he was betrayed and arrested. He did so on the night before he was scourged and crucified. Jesus sacrificed everything. He did all of this because he loves us. We who are crucified in Christ *"live by faith in the Son of God."* By his Holy Spirit, our guide, we find the strength to humbly give ourselves to God and others.

Using the WITH Compass–Humble

To walk humbly with our God is a necessary part of our journey. And it can be easier said than done, so we need a guide. The purpose of the WITH Compass is to encourage you to ask the Holy Spirit to assess the level of humility you have in your heart for God and others.

Keeping your humility in mind, ask the Holy Spirit these questions as they pertain to you becoming more Christ-like:

- Where am I at this moment?
- Where do I go from here?

The Holy Spirit may humble you of your pride in some aspect of your life. Or he may show you where you need to defer to others more humbly. You may hear God's Spirit encouraging you to continue to put God and others before yourself. The key is to listen with an open and submissive posture that allows God to transform you. By becoming familiar and comfortable with this tool, we can stay oriented toward God, remaining humble as we allow him to navigate for us on our journey.

Capture Your Moment

Asking God for humility can be a scary proposition. But not asking to be humbled may be even worse. The Holy Spirit humbles the proud. Which approach do you prefer to take? Why?

Humble Prayer

Paul's letters give us great insight into a man who remained humble while God used him to do great things for his Kingdom. His statement in Galatians provides a wonderfully humble prayer centered on Jesus' most lovingly humble act:

> **"I have been crucified with Christ; yet I live, no longer I, but Christ lives in me; insofar as I now live in the flesh, I live by faith in the Son of God who has loved me and given himself up for me. "**
> **Galatians 2:20**

Having traveled through each of the four WITH Compass points, you're now more familiar with it as a tool to help you stay oriented to God and to navigate with him. The key is to allow the Holy Spirit to be your guide in this and in all things. How you use this tool is up to you and your guide—the Holy Spirit.

When I speak to groups about this topic I lead them through a prayer that encompasses all of the WITH Compass points. Perhaps *The WITH Prayer* will be helpful to you on your journey:

The WITH Prayer

Welcome the Holy Spirit with an open heart, mind and body. Express your desire to be guided by the Holy Spirit by praying *The WITH Prayer*. Open your hands to receive the Spirit as a gift.

- Come, Holy Spirit. Fill me.
- Holy Spirit, show me where I am being willful.
  Make my heart willing.

- Holy Spirit, show me where I am blocking intimacy to you. Help me to be intimate.
- Holy Spirit, show me where I lack trust. Give me the courage to trust you.
- Holy Spirit, show me where I lack humility. Keep me humble.
- I embrace you, Holy Spirit, as the guide for my journey.
- Thank you, Holy Spirit, for drawing me ever closer to you, my God.
- In Jesus' name I pray. Amen.

WITH God

Journeying with God and entrusting our lives to the guidance of his Holy Spirit actually frees us to willingly live according to God's plan. As we grow in our intimate relationship with God, we better understand his ways. As we trust in God's providential will, we humbly submit to his plans for our lives. In doing so, we become the people he created us to be.

It is imperative that we keep in mind that our destination is not a physical place but a person. Knowing that person, God the Father, the Son and the Holy Spirit—three in one—is our destination. That is why this is a journey unlike any other. It is a way of living—an ongoing, transformational journey.

We cannot expect everything to be made clear at once. We live in a GPS world. But we need to navigate through it with a compass. We need to accept the fact that God is not going to give us step by step instructions to a specific destination. We also need to know that the timing of events in our lives is not driven by our desires. In fact, we do not have control over most things in our lives. God's plans will dictate just how fast or far we will travel. We need to embrace his way of life as our own.

The WITH Compass is a guidance tool. The Holy Spirit is our true guide. He will orient us and navigate for us as we seek to be willing, intimate, trusting and humble with God each and every day. With the Holy Spirit as our guide, we can use the WITH Compass for our journey of a lifetime...WITH God.

GOD

Our Portraits of God

We like to tease Joshua about his first family drawings. Josh is very talented in many ways. He is an excellent student, a naturally gifted athlete and quite the stage performer. However, his artistic ability, shall we say, is not his strongest talent. Here is my favorite drawing of the two of us that he created as a four-year-old.

Joshua and Dad circa 2002

That's me on the left, back when I still had hair! The significance of our "hands" touching is not lost on me. I treasure this piece of childhood art. Many parents cover their refrigerators with these family portraits. They are valued, not because of their

123

artistic beauty or accuracy, but because of the love and sense of belonging they represent. This is one way that children seek to express their identity as a family member.

We form our own "portraits" of God in a similar way. However, our portraits can't possibly represent the Trinitarian Christian God—consisting of three persons in one being—who we know as the Father, Son and Holy Spirit. In other words, we will never know what God truly "looks like" in this lifetime. Any portrait we might create will surely fall far short of God. But does that really matter? Does God think any less of us because we are, at best, childish artists trying to reproduce something that really can't be captured in human terms? What matters is that we identify with God, so that we can relate to him and journey with him.

Joshua's drawing still captures my heart because I know that he was expressing his connection to me as well as his love for me. In the same way, we capture a little piece of God's heart each time we seek to connect with him and express our love for him. Each of us has our own unique image of God. However, these images are at best incomplete, and at worst downright inaccurate. Therefore, we must continually pursue God in order to know him better. As we journey with God, our image, perception and understanding of him mature, and ultimately, this deepens our relationship with him.

God's Image Revealed

When we intentionally choose to journey with God, we embark on a journey like no other. It is a journey of encounter. It is a journey not to a physical destination, but to a person: *God*. We encounter the same God who created us in *"our image, after our likeness."*

The writers of the Bible sought to capture the essence of God in their words. Artists throughout the centuries have sought to paint and sculpt the image of God. These images and the

124

countless others like them embody our human desire to express our knowledge of God. They demonstrate our human attempt to depict God as we perceive his image and likeness to be.

The best depiction of that image and likeness is found in the man who walked the arid hills and valleys of Israel over 2,000 years ago. Jesus' incarnation, his taking on flesh, provides us with a tangible human image of God.

> *And the Word became flesh and made his dwelling among us, and **we saw** his glory, the glory as of the Father's only Son, full of grace and truth.*
> *John 1:14 (Emphasis added.)*

In this passage we see a distinctive description of what it means to "see" God the Father's glory. John makes it clear that God the Father is revealed in his Son, Jesus.

> *No one has ever seen God. The only Son, God, who is at the Father's side, has revealed him.*   *John 1:18*

Jesus, fully human, embodied the reality that in our humanity, we were created in God's image and likeness. God the Father sent his Son, which allows us to relate to him in the most human of ways. In the act of stepping through the gate that is Jesus, we immediately envision God differently. He becomes our Savior and the Lord of our lives, and we begin to put away our "childish" images of him. This will be an ongoing process and we can look to our WITH Compass to explore a deeper relationship with God by the power of the Holy Spirit. It is the Holy Spirit who illuminates our understanding of God, like an art expert who helps us to understand and appreciate the different aspects of a painted masterpiece. The Holy Spirit reveals to us the ever-changing and expanding ways of God as we continue to journey with him.

Capture Your Moment

How has your image of God changed as you've read through this book? How has your image of God changed throughout your life?

God's Image of Us

Let's shift our focus from our images of God to how God imagines us to be. Imagine a painting being created. The artist has a clear image in his mind of what the final painting looks like. In the beginning, the painter's easel stands holding a large blank canvas.

The first strokes of the master's brush lay the foundations that may not be seen when the painting is complete. Layers of colors are lovingly applied. Occasionally something appears on the canvas that doesn't seem to make sense until additional colors and brush strokes bring into focus a powerful new image. This process continues time and again...

Imagine that this painting is being created by God. One tangible way to do so would be to read through the detailed descriptions of creation in Genesis. In that text we can envision God as the artist and creator of all things: light, the heavens and the earth, land and sea, day and night, and all the creatures of the earth. The Bible provides us with many images of God's

127

people. In the Old Testament we journey from the creation of Adam and Eve to their beautiful dwelling place in the garden, to Abraham's climb up Mount Moriah to sacrifice his son Isaac. We follow the Israelites from slavery in Egypt to freedom as they wandered in the desert, eventually crossing into the Promised Land. In the New Testament God's image takes us through the sites throughout ancient Israel like the Sea of Galilee, the Mount of Olives and Solomon's Temple.

God, with great foresight, envisioned all of these people and places in his "painting." Jesus, the Messiah, appears in all of these images in the great artist's painting—both indirectly and directly. In the Old Testament his coming was foreshadowed and prophesized, while in the New Testament he was revealed. In one sense, this painting that God has created is as much a portrait as it is a scene. At its focal point, the painting is a person, not a place. It is Jesus! God's image captures Jesus' birth, death and resurrection in the same painting, and you and I have also been placed in this grand design.

The ancient form of mosaic art, reinvented, provides us with a way to envision this. Perhaps you've seen one of those images that from a distance is very clear, but as you look more closely, you realize there is more to it. The larger image is made up of innumerable smaller images or photographs. I once saw an image of Jesus created this way. It was made up of smaller images of people. People of all shapes, sizes, colors and ages. Those people actually were the body of Christ. How cool!

In his first letter to the Corinthians, Paul uses the analogy of a body that helps us to imagine how we have been placed in this "image" of Christ.

> ...**God has placed each part in the body just as he wanted it to be**. *If all the parts were the same, how could there be a body? As it is, there are many parts. But there is only one body.*

*Now you are the body of Christ, and **each one of you is
a part of it**. 1 Corinthians 12:18-20, 27
(Emphasis added.)*

Paul's imagery helps us see that we are all members of
Christ's body, his church. In belonging to the church, we have
the opportunity to be nurtured and to grow in our faith. As we
do so, we begin to find ways that we can actively participate in
the mission of the body of Christ.

When we journey with God it is always important to keep
our focus on the painter (God the Father), the central figure of
the painting (Jesus the Son), and the guide (God's Holy Spirit),
who helps us to embrace who we were created to be as well
as to understand our part in God's painting. This redirects our
attention away from our incomplete and inaccurate images of
God from our past. It turns our focus toward God as he continues
to reveal himself and his purposes. Over time, our image of God
continues to grow as we experience him along the way. While
our image of God is changing, his image of us never does. It is his
image of us that we want to understand and appreciate.

God Sees Our Potential

Earlier, I shared the story of the moment that I surrendered
my business to God. Back then, I had been a part of a collaborative effort to write a book called *The Sales Coach*. My chapter
was on time management, a topic on which I had done a great
deal of speaking, training and coaching. Interestingly, shortly
before I had been asked to write the chapter, I had changed my
entire way of thinking about time management. While coaching
individuals on the tried and true time management techniques
and strategies, it occurred to me that different people embraced
them differently. This was driven home to me even more clearly

as I observed how Maria and I used these techniques in profoundly different ways.

With a degree in Industrial Engineering, Maria embraced the structured elements of traditional time management. (She still does today.) I, on the other hand, did not. There is a reason why I do not have a degree in engineering. I am not a logical thinker, and no matter how hard I tried to be structured and disciplined in managing my time, I just got frustrated. This epiphany, that Maria and I think and function differently, helped me to accept that it was okay for me to manage my time differently than her. I stopped forcing myself to do something that did not come naturally to me, and I began to develop a "time management" mindset that worked for me. Perhaps more importantly, I began to view my own way of being in a more positive light. I had always beat myself up for not being like Maria and others who were "good" at managing their time and who subsequently seemed to be more productive.

This realization prompted me to head in an entirely new direction for my business. Instead of focusing on the narrow topic of time management I broadened my view to the concept of potential. This new focus led to changes in my presentations, workshops and coaching. It also prompted a new descriptive tag-line for my business: "...to understand, develop and realize your potential."

My time management epiphany was something that came from within me. Back then, I began to accept my uniqueness and to appreciate that I had my own way of being and doing. This was all "hardwired" into me, and I understood that I had to stop trying to be someone I wasn't—a false self.

This all happened before I committed my life to Christ. Looking back on it now, I realize that I was living my life out of my God-given potential despite the fact that I wasn't "living for and working with" God yet. Who knew that almost 25 years later I would be writing another book about God-given potential? God did!

There have been several questions that I've wrestled with since I began writing *Our Journey WITH God.* "How will this book about a journey with God end?" and "Where do I go from here?" First, I have to acknowledge that I've never felt worthy of writing about God. The creator of all things, God is so much more than I have a capacity to know and understand. (See Joshua's portrait above.) Second, it seems to me that a book about a journey with God doesn't really have an ending, at least not in a traditional sense. By its very definition, a journey with God is ongoing, right on into eternity. Third, you and I don't have the answers about our individual journeys with God, let alone our journey's end, but God does!

The answers to my questions have emerged over time. One aspect of my current ministry is to coach people who are seeking greater self-understanding and direction in life. My job as a coach is to help the person I'm coaching understand their God-given talents and motivations. This isn't like coaching a sport where the athlete is being instructed in a specific skill. It is more an exercise in drawing out what is already within the person, having been placed there by God. My job as a coach is simply to act as a guide.

At times the insights people receive strike like lightning in an epiphany of understanding. Other insights dawn gently by revealing the beginnings of something more. Answers to many questions that people have about their identity come at the same time that new questions are being raised. It is awesome to know that God is behind these insights, and I am blessed to see this happen for the people I coach.

This is where I found my answers as to how to finish this book. We find our "ending" where it began, in God. Knowing him and his purposes helps us to know ourselves. Our willingness to seek God's design within ourselves provides us with insight into how we were created. And so... the end of this book is intended to help you on your ongoing journey with God.

Capture Your Moment

What insights has God given you about your past that point to your potential? How might you appreciate your potential more? Describe what it might mean to you to know that God has always had plans for you?

You are called to live as the person you were created to be. You are an unrepeatable onceness, God's masterpiece! We are all unique and will live out our Christian journey in our own unique way. As we seek to become Christ-like, we can expect that we will do so differently from others. This is all a part of our lifelong journey from a false identity to our God-intended true identity. However, this authenticity can be overshadowed by the expectations of a world that emphasizes the need for us to be "productive".

Being and Doing

This worldly "productivity" mentality can challenge us on our journey with God. The primary starting point and emphasis of our journey must always focus on knowing and being with God, not just doing for God. Knowing what we are supposed to be doing for God will always be a question for us. This was an issue for Jesus' disciples as they sought to understand what they were supposed to do for God.

So they said to him, "What can we do to accomplish the works of God?" Jesus answered and said to them, "This is the work of God, that you believe in the one he sent."
John 6:28-29

Jesus clearly emphasizes believing in him is the starting point for God's works. This is not to say that we shouldn't do things for God, but knowing him is our first priority. As we come to know God, in Christ, we understand ourselves as he created us to be—our identity. This helps us to gain clarity in what he's calling us to do for him—our purpose. The WITH Compass with its directional questions, "Where am I?" and "Where am I going?" helps us to turn our attention to God's guide, the Holy Spirit. The key is that God initiates it all!

Keeping our priorities aligned can help us to avoid the trap of becoming busy for God while losing sight of our relationship with him. Being precedes doing. Once we walk through the gate that is Christ and our identity in him changes, we then want to do as he did.

For to this you have been called, because Christ also suffered for you, leaving you an example that you should follow in his footsteps.
1 Peter 2:21

We are called to follow in Christ's footsteps. But we will all do so in our own way. We will now journey into your authentic identity (being) and unique purpose (doing) in Christ, keeping in mind that God has insights ready and waiting for you. Oh, and by the way, don't forget to bring your WITH Compass!

Discovering Our Authentic Identity

From the beginning, we as individual masterpieces, sons and daughters of God, are smaller images in the most grand and beautiful image ever created.

For you created my inmost being; you knit me together in my mother's womb. I praise you because I am fearfully and wonderfully made; your works are wonderful, I know that full well. Psalm 139:13-14

By embracing this truth that we are created uniquely by God, we begin to see more clearly how we fit into his "painting." The painter knows us as his subjects better than we know ourselves. Envisioning God's view of us is critical to our growth in him.

Maria and I often reflect on how significant events in the lives of our children gave us glimpses into their true identities. When Joey was five years old, we signed him up to play soccer in our community program. On the first day of practice we divided the group into two teams, and they began to scrimmage. Within a few minutes, Joey had scored several goals. A short time later he was up to five. We put him on defense to keep from running up the score any further. Even on defense he proceeded to dribble the ball the length of the field through both teams to score more goals, seven in all!

At the end of practice the father of another child asked me if Joey was my son and when I said, "Yes," he responded, "He's intense!" It wasn't what I had expected him to say. I was proud and a little embarrassed at the same time because Joey had been so dominant. Back then we thought we might have had a soccer prodigy on our hands. While Joey turned out to be a pretty good

134

soccer player, what we truly glimpsed that day was his natural intensity, energy and vision.

When Sarah was seven years old, she created a structure out of colorful blocks that awed us in its intricacy, balance and beauty. We were amazed that she had created this by herself, without instructions! We caught a glimpse of Sarah's authentic creative ability that day.

As a five-year-old, Joshua used to give us a play-by-play account of his backyard baseball and basketball games. He still loves to give play-by-play explanations of his athletic exploits in college. Josh has an innate ability to explain intricate activities with great detail and enthusiasm.

The reason I share our children's stories of authentic identity is because in children we see a purity and innocence that is often lost as we get older. Children do things because they want to do them. They choose to be in the moment, with the primary motivation of enjoying themselves. Because we need to be productive as adults, our motivations obviously and legitimately shift. However, the experience of "growing up" can lead us on a path that isn't always ideally suited for us. I shared my own experience of burning out and getting sick while working in a job that was misaligned with my authentic talents. Perhaps you've had a similar experience. That is why being aware of and attending to our authentic self is so important.

Our authentic identity has always been there, but it is often hidden away. That is why reminiscing about favorite childhood activities elicits a positive response in adults. Watch the unbridled joy of someone talking about their favorite activities as a kid. I begin a lot of my talks and retreats with the question, "What was your favorite childhood activity?" It's fun to listen and watch as participants relive their childhood experiences. More than once I've heard people excitedly say, "This weekend I'm going to... (fill in childhood activity)."

Think of an instance when you have been passionately engaged in something that has brought you great energy. Time seemed to fly by as you got lost in what you were doing. These often joyful experiences provide a glimpse of your authentic identity as God created you to be.

Capture Your Moment

What was your favorite childhood activity? How did that activity reveal some of your authentic identity? How might knowing that God uniquely created you affect your perception of your life as a journey with God? How might this understanding of your glimpse, as God's masterpiece, affect the way you journey with him into the future?

On our journey with God, we continually discover more of who he created us to be—our authentic identity. We also begin to find a greater desire to pursue his unique purpose for our life. Put simply, authentic identity leads to unique purpose. As we grow in our own loving and serving relationship with God, we will see further glimpses of his intended purpose for us.

136

Pursuing Our Unique Purpose

Purpose can be defined as the reason for which something is done or created or for which something exists. Paul's words to the Ephesian church makes it clear that God created us for a reason:

> *For we are God's masterpiece. He has created us anew*
> *in Christ Jesus, so we can do the good things He planned*
> *for us long ago.*   *Ephesians 2:10*

Stop and think about that for a minute. You are *"God's masterpiece"*, what I've been referring to as authentic identity. Don't forget, we're talking about *God*—the creator and ruler of the universe! When you choose to walk through Jesus, the gate, God creates you anew—for his purposes! How's that for the reason for which you exist?

God lovingly created us for a purpose. Figuring out God's unique purpose for our lives is often a challenging part of our journey with him. We will need to embrace the ever-changing, sometimes difficult nature inherent in our journey. We need to know that this will be an ongoing, life-long process. In many ways, God will continue to be a mystery to us, but we still need to pursue an ever-deepening relationship with him. Being in a loving relationship with God tends to give us a new perspective on our experiences. That is why glimpses of our unique purpose are found in many of life's experiences.

Each glimpse that we had of our children's authentic identity was like watching God add brush strokes to his canvas. We look forward to who our children are becoming, as God continues to reveal his plans for their lives.

At this point on his journey, Joey works as an eighth-grade math teacher whose intensity and energy is infectious. I was unaware that on the day I wrote the story about Joey's seven-goal soccer practice, he was conducting tryouts for his school's eighth-grade boys' soccer team. Joey was pleasantly surprised that a large number of boys had shown up for tryouts. In years past, the school had barely had the eleven players needed to field a team. Even though Joey was only starting his second year of teaching and his first-ever coaching job, these boys had naturally been drawn to him. They had caught a glimpse of Joey's God-given passion and wanted to be a part of his team.

As his dad, it is a joy for me to think of the impact Joey is having as he pursues his calling to teach and coach underprivileged, inner-city kids. He loves his work. He does so, because while becoming the man he was created to be, he also recognizes the significant impact he is having on his young students.

In Sarah's case, I thought, "Maybe Sarah should be an architect." She isn't! And I am perfectly fine with that because I have come to trust in God's "parental" plan for her life, not mine. As Sarah has grown and matured, we have continually seen her unique talent for balancing beauty with order. Sarah is a budding entrepreneur with a calligraphy and hand-lettering business that people have been raving about.

We often wondered if Josh might consider becoming a sports broadcaster because of his ability to explain the intricacies of all the activity that happens in a sporting event. Instead, he relies on his unique, God-given talent to help others understand complex subject matter as a successful chemistry tutor in college. As of this writing, we're looking forward to Josh pursuing his own unique path as he graduates from college.

Joey, Sarah and Joshua are each pursuing their own unique purposes in life. Consider that this coming together of identity and purpose is God continuing to put brush to canvas in their life stories. God is doing the same in your life, too.

God will give us "glimpses" of his painting along the way that will point to our God-intended purpose. As we continue to discover our authentic identity, we will also learn of our unique purpose through time. There will be times when we "see" God acting in our lives. And in these grace-filled moments when God reveals himself, we are changed. This often manifests as an almost indescribable stirring from deep within us to do something for God. This desire wells up in response to our interaction with God.

> *Find your delight in the LORD who will give you your heart's desire.*   Psalm 37:4

As we focus our attention on God, we find that our desire is to live for him, according to his will. This is because the desire originates in him. That is when we begin to live out God's purpose for our lives.

Capture Your Moment

What glimpses of your unique purpose have been demonstrated by your authentic talents? How might your life's experiences point to God's intended purpose for you?

A Purposeful Journey

Even as you read these words, God continues to add new color to his canvas for your life. Some additions bring clarity, while other "events" blur the image. Some parts of the image can be disturbing until later on, when we see God's hand at work through them. In the **Trusting** section of the WITH Compass, we explored the concept that we need to trust that "things," good and bad, have a purpose:

We know that all things work for good for those who love God, who are called according to his purpose.
Romans 8:28

There is purpose in many things, even though we may not fully understand what that purpose is. Regardless of what is going on around us, we must always remember that God is present with us on our journey, and he is in control—no matter what! On our journey, things will happen to us personally, to those we know and love, and in the world in general. Remembering that God is in control gives us the perspective that everything will work out in the end. God knows what the finished painting looks like.

If we are submitting to God's will for our lives, we don't necessarily need to worry about what the painting of our lives is going to look like. The details of this image don't really matter. The presence of the painter in our lives is the key! This shift in our perspective from future to present is critical to our journey with God. It allows us to focus on our relationship with all three persons of the Trinity. In that relationship, we will continue to develop our understanding of our authentic identity and subsequently, our unique purpose.

We need to be aware that our fleshly desires may lead us down a different path. Satan will always be at work in creating doubt with his lies, which are intended to confuse and mislead us. Using the WITH Compass to seek the Holy Spirit's guidance can keep us on God's path.

We live in a world that pressures us to attain for ourselves and to achieve success in our own strength. The expectation in our GPS-guided world is that every step must be planned out to ensure our success. But God does not give us step-by-step instructions with a clear destination. He guides us by his Spirit, allowing us to make our choices each and every day. That is why our journey with God is always going to be a purposeful one.

A Fruitful Journey

Jesus, having completed the purpose of his earthly life, gave his disciples a very clear purpose of their own:

> *Then Jesus approached and said to them, "All power in heaven and on earth has been given to me. Go, therefore, and make disciples of all nations, baptizing them in the name of the Father, and of the Son, and of the holy Spirit, teaching them to observe all that I have commanded you. And behold, I am with you always, until the end of the age."* Matthew 28:18-20

What better place to find our purpose? As he ascended back to heaven to sit at his Father's right hand, Jesus gave a very clear directive: *"Go..."* Of course, we need to go! We are on a journey. Jesus expects us to make disciples, baptizing and teaching them to observe all he commanded. Wow, that's a lot of purpose!

This isn't to suggest that each of us are going to do all of these things. Our journey is meant to give us the opportunity to understand our authentic identity (being) and unique purpose (doing) so that we can respond to Jesus' command to go. As members of the body of Christ, we all have a unique way, directed by God's Spirit, to be and do.

Some people are called to full-time ministry, but many are not. However, we *are* all called to full-time relationship with God! This concept of unique purpose is more about how we will live out our authentic identity for God. For example, your unique purpose today might be to reach out to someone who is down, to smile at someone who is hurting or to give to someone in need. Regardless of our "ministry" role, we can expect that living out our unique purpose in Christ will have an impact on the world around us. In fact, Paul spoke of our purpose in this way:

> *The fruit of the Spirit is love, joy, peace, patience, kindness, generosity, faithfulness, gentleness, self-control.*
> *Galatians 5:22-23*

When we journey with God and his Holy Spirit, we will see fruit. We must go and be fruitful with the Holy Spirit's guidance. One way we will know that we are living in God's intended, unique purpose is by the fruit we see along the way.

We don't want to get caught up in trying to figure out how we are going to be true to Jesus' command to go. We are not meant to do so in our own strength. The Holy Spirit is our guide and Jesus must be our source:

> *I am the vine, you are the branches. Whoever remains*
> *in me and I in him will bear much fruit, because without*
> *me you can do nothing.* *John 15:5*

We need to remain in him. Use the WITH Compass to help you do so. By remaining in **intimate** connection with Jesus, we desire to **do his will**, **trusting** in him to see us through as we seek to **humbly** serve him. I encourage you to look to your guide, the Holy Spirit, and watch him bear fruit through you.

Capture Your Moment

When have you seen God impact another person through you? In what way might that fruitful experience have pointed to your unique purpose? How might the WITH Compass help you to stay on track in your pursuit of God and his purpose for your life?

Are We There Yet?

A friend of mine gave me some great advice when our children were little. Every time one of his children asked how long before they arrived at their destination, his answer was the same: "Ten minutes." I used the same technique and knew it was working when one of the older kids answered Joshua's innocent five-year-old inquiry with, "Don't ask him, Josh. He's just going to say ten minutes." Our adult children still roll their eyes when you ask them about my persistence in answering their question so consistently. Of course, it's easy to understand the impatience of a child who is strapped into a car seat. But stop and think about how we exhibit the same behavior. It's human nature to want to know where we are going and when we're going to get there. I know I've felt that way at times on my journey with God. Writing this book over the past five years has been quite a journey. There have been many times when, wanting to know when I might finish the book, I asked, "Are we there yet, Lord?" It is okay to ask, by the way. But it's more important to wait on his answer.

That is why the travel question, so often voiced from the back seat of the family car, is so instructive. "Are we there yet?" No and yes. No, we have not reached our final destination, eternal life with God. Yes, we are "there" if we embrace God as our destination in the present, each and every day.

Hope for the Journey

Remaining focused on God and living in the moment with him is what *Our Journey WITH God* is about.

First, **Our**... It is of paramount importance to our journey that we understand the meaning of being created in "our" image and likeness.

Journey... Entering into a relationship with God and journeying with him changes everything. We are redeemed in him and called to become more Christ-like on our journey with him.

WITH... This is where we live day to day with God's Spirit as our guide, using our WITH Compass to be willing, intimate, trusting and humble. The Holy Spirit helps us to remain oriented toward him in all we do ("Where am I?") as we seek to navigate through life with God ("Where am I going?"). In him we continue to grow in our unique God-given identity as we seek to live like Jesus. As we do, our purpose in life becomes clearer as we live in his love and extend his love to others.

As always, we come back to **God**... Regardless of what is happening around us and in us, God is always there. Whether he is allowing a period of trial and suffering, an opportunity to selflessly serve, a time of dryness and perceived distance from him, or a momentary glimpse of his glory, God is there. If we embrace him and don't dwell on our circumstances, God's peace will be upon us. By keeping God's bigger "painting" in mind, we learn to get beyond ourselves to that destination that is God. This helps us to stop worrying about our circumstances in the moment and to focus on God, who is the true destination of our journey. We can trust in Jesus' promise that God is in control and that he is always there, in us and with us.

Paul expressed this idea of living in the moment for God with hope for his ultimate destination:

> *If I go on living in the flesh, that means fruitful labor for me. And I do not know which I shall choose. I am caught between the two. I long to depart this life and be with Christ, [for] that is far better. Yet that I remain [in] the flesh is more necessary for your benefit. And this **I know with confidence**, that I shall remain and continue in the service of all of you for your progress and joy in the faith.*   *Philippians 1:22-23 (Emphasis added.)*

This is what it means to faithfully journey with God. Paul knew with confidence that as he journeyed with God, his purpose was to give himself to God and to love and serve others for God. Of course, he also looked forward to that time when he would be with Christ. In Paul's confident words, we hear the embrace of a journey that isn't always clearly defined. We too must embrace our shared journey with God, trusting each and every day that he is there with us. While Paul's is one of the best-known stories of what it means to journey with God, we need not be like Paul. The only one we want to be like is Jesus—and the Holy Spirit is going to guide us in that effort in our own authentic way. Finally, Paul offers us the hope of a race well run:

> *I have competed well; I have finished the race; I have kept the faith. From now on the crown of righteousness*

awaits me, which the Lord, the just judge, will award to
me on that day, and not only to me, but to all who have
longed for his appearance.   *2 Timothy 4:7-8*

The journey ends in God, just as it began. Our journey's destination is to be with him forever. God is our destination, now and forever!

I have one last story to share with you. It is the story of your future. You have chosen to journey with God. Along the way you've experienced many ups and downs and twists and turns. There have been joys and sorrows. You have done your best to seek God first in all things. At times you've failed, but you've turned back to him, seeking his forgiveness. You've come to trust in the Holy Spirit as your guide, and he has led you to a deeper, more beautiful and loving relationship with God and others. Now, imagine that moment when you finish your race, when "forever" begins and Jesus speaks these words to you:

Well done, my good and faithful servant. Matthew 25:21

Imagine knowing God deeply as he truly is, Father, Son and Spirit. Imagine feeling unconditionally loved by God and completely affirmed by him for who you are. Trust that God looks forward to that moment as well.

My prayer for you is captured in Paul's letter to the Philippians:

I am confident of this, that the one who began a good
work in you will continue to complete it until the day of
Christ Jesus.   *Philippians 1:6*

May you come to know your authentic identity and unique purpose in Christ as you persevere in the race that is...

Our Journey WITH God!

CAPTURE YOUR MOMENT circa TODAY!

Our Journey WITH God!

CAPTURE YOUR MOMENT circa TODAY!

ABOUT THE AUTHOR

J oe Killian was born and raised in Pittsburgh, Pennsylvania. After receiving a Bachelor of Science in Business Administration from Indiana University of Pennsylvania, Joe began his career as a corporate recruiter and training and development specialist. He then received a Master of Business Administration from the University of Pittsburgh's Katz Graduate School of Business. Upon completing his MBA, Joe embarked on a successful venture as a professional speaker, trainer, consultant and coach for clients such as Merrill Lynch, Verizon, Xerox, Alcoa, United Way, US Attorney's Office and Promotional Products Association International. Sensing God's call, Joe went back to school, receiving a Ministerial License from Greater Works Outreach Bible School and then completing a Master of Arts in Religious Education at Duquesne University. Joe worked as a Director of Religious Education in the Pittsburgh and Greensburg Dioceses of the Catholic Church for more than ten years. Now, through his ministry, Joe provides guidance to those seeking to enhance their journey with God. He does so as an author, speaker, retreat leader and coach. Joe is married to Maria, his best friend and wife of over thirty years. They reside in Oakmont, Pennsylvania, where they raised three wonderful children, Joey, Sarah and Joshua. Visit Joe at www.joekillian.com to learn more about his ministry.

CPSIA information can be obtained
at www.ICGtesting.com
Printed in the USA
BVHW081809290819
556975BV00006B/14/P